Ahimsa Dog Training Manual

A Practical, Force-Free Guide to Problem Solving and Manners

Also by
Grisha Stewart, MA, CPDT-KA, KPACTP

*Behavior Adjustment Training: BAT for Aggression,
Frustration and Fear in Dogs* (Book)

Intro to BAT (DVD)

Organic Socialization: BAT for Aggression & Fear in Dogs
(DVD)

BATting 1000: Two-Day Seminar (DVD)

*Give Your Puppy a Choice: Modern Socialization and
Training* (DVD)

Current titles are available through
FunctionalRewards.com

The *Official* Ahimsa Dog Training Manual

A Practical, Force-Free Guide to Problem Solving and Manners

Grisha Stewart, MA, CPDT-KA, KPACTP

Published by Ahimsa Dog Training, LLC
Seattle, WA

The Official Ahimsa Dog Training Manual
A Practical, Force-Free Guide to Problem Solving and Manners
Grisha Stewart, M.A., CPDT-KA, KPACTP

Published by Ahimsa Dog Training, LLC
902 NW 49th Street
Seattle, WA, 98107 USA
206-364-4072
www.DoggieZen.com / info@doggiezen.com
© 2007, 2012, 2013 Grisha Stewart

4th Edition

Graphic design: Grisha Stewart (basic illustrations) and Lili Chin (the cute ones)
Cover photos: Alyssa Rose Photography
Interior photographs: Rachel Butler, Janet Graham, Merijeanne Hollingsworth, Diane Kasperowicz, Aaron Lieberman, Rodrigo Lima, Susan McKeon, Almudena Novo, Anna Nussey, Michal Pregowski, Steven Swanson, Cheryl Viera, Tonya Wilhelm, and Kirby Wycoff

ISBN-13 978-1478176411
ISBN-10 1478176415

Praise for *The* Official *Ahimsa Dog Training Manual*:

🐾 From puppyhood to learning theory, Grisha has done what she does best: take complicated subjects and make them easy to follow and simple to understand. For pet parents, this book is a nice foundation book to take their puppies and dogs toward being a "Canine good citizen," and helps problem-solve some of the most common issues that are presented to trainers and behavior experts regularly.

Beyond the basic manners instructions, this guide also touches on fear and reactivity; offering help to the average person so they can begin teaching skills that will lay the building blocks toward a happier and more relaxed dog.

Finally, this is a great guide for rescues to give to adopters, and for trainers to hand to their clients; all with the goal of helping dogs live in peace and harmony with their humans, and visa versa.

The *Ahimsa Dog Training Manual* is a must for any pet parent's bookshelf and a bonus for trainers to get, yet another publication by Grisha.

Nan Arthur, CDBC, CPDT-KSA, KPACTP/Faculty, author of *Chill Out Fido! How to Calm Your Dog*

🐾 Of the thousands of dog training books out there, it's rare finding one that has something new to say or presents the science of positive training in a unique and meaningful way. Grisha's new booklet, the *Ahimsa Dog Training Manual*, does just that. Clear, concise, informative and extremely user-friendly, this book deserves a prominent place on every trainer's bookshelf.

Paul Owens, Best-selling author of *The Dog Whisperer; A Compassionate, Nonviolent Approach to Dog Training* and *The Puppy Whisperer: A Compassionate, Nonviolent Guide to Early Training and Care.*

This book is a great resource for anyone interesting in understanding, or increasing their understanding of low stress, force-free handling and training techniques. Pet owners will find it a useful primer for developing a positive and trusting relationship with their dog. If there's something you want your dog to do, or stop doing, there's a good chance that this book addresses it.

Debbie Jacobs, CPDT-KA, CAP2, author of *A Guide to Living With and Training a Fearful Dog*

This is it! This is the easy-to-read, concise handbook that every responsible dog owner will want to read. This manual spells out practical, step-by-step training solutions while educating the reader on the science behind the theory. Grisha is the leading authority on Behavior Adjustment Training (BAT), and shares her unique method to bring about change in a positive, force-free, and fear-free environment. She shows us a new way to teach loose-leash walking; one that is free from frustration and maps a clear strategy for us to follow. The dog world is grateful to Grisha for taking time out of her busy schedule to give us this wonderful resource.

Kyra Sundance, renowned Stunt Dog Performer and author of *101 Dog Tricks*

"When Fido arrives at the intersection of Good Dog Street and Bad Dog Alley, which way will he go?" asks Grisha Stewart in her book, *The Official Ahimsa Dog Training Manual*. Grisha's book can help you manage Fido's environment and train him to make good choices. She offers a variety of force-free ways to train common behaviors, and her writing is always engaging and as friendly as her methods. Your dog will definitely enjoy your training sessions based on this book.

Teoti Anderson, CPDT-KA, KPA-CTP, author of *Puppy Care and Training* and *Your Outta Control Puppy: How to Turn Your Precocious Pup Into a Perfect Pet* and Past President of the Association of Pet Dog Trainers

GREAT resource for puppy buyers! It gives the basics for everything a dog needs to learn in easy-to-understand terms. Breeders should use it in their puppy packet! Can I get them in bulk?

Michel Berner, Viszla breeder

For Steve and Spoon,

*Who helped me catch the dog training bug
and devote my life to helping dogs and people
understand each other.*

Special thanks to the brilliant and creative staff,
devoted volunteers, and passionate students at
Ahimsa Dog Training in Seattle.

Thanks to all of those who contributed photos (see page 4 for names).
Thanks to Ann Allums, Xaviara Augenblick, Sara Boyle, Dana Gallagher,
Anne Humphreys, Casey Lomanaco, La Trenda S. Walker, Liz Wyant, and
Kirby Wycoff for their careful proofreading.
Any remaining errors are, of course, all mine!

Introduction

I object to violence because when it appears to do good, the good is only
temporary; the evil it does is permanent.
—Mahatma Ghandi

This book is the training manual for Ahimsa Dog Training in Seattle. "Ahimsa" is a Buddhist doctrine of nonviolence to all living things, reflecting our focus on force-free dog training and behavior modification. At Ahimsa, we focus on using progressive, science-based training to build two-way communication between humans and their dogs.

You will learn to be a consistent, calm, force-free coach for your puppy or adult dog. These techniques work whether your dog is a puppy, a new-to-you rescue dog, or a dog you have had for many years. You can even apply this exact same training to cats, horses, ferrets, mice, and any other animals that eat (that would be all of them), although you may need to train for briefer periods with your cat or snapping turtle, because they don't have the patience that dogs do! So when I refer to your dog in this book, feel free to think of another animal instead.

My hope is that you will not only use this book to teach your dog new behaviors and fix problems, but also begin to see a new way to interact with your dog—and maybe even apply this new vision to the people around you. Once you start looking for the positive side of your dog's behavior, you may find that you do the same with your children, partner, and coworkers. Focusing more on behavior and consequences, rather than character flaws, helps us understand where the dog or other person is coming from. For example, your dog is not a bad or dominant dog; there is just some behavior that needs to be changed to live together in peace.

If you are having issues with aggression or there is danger in any way from your dog, please see a force-free professional dog trainer or behaviorist and check out my book on BAT. The training tips in this manual still apply to your situation, and there is a section on BAT in this book, but you probably need some more substantial and details advice to keep everyone safe.

This manual goes well with group training classes, even if you aren't taking them with us at Ahimsa. If you have a puppy, please attend a force-free puppy class and/or systematically help your puppy encounter new people, dogs, surfaces, etc. in fun ways. This book covers a lot of the training you will need, but nothing replaces the chance to meet other dogs and people during the very important socialization period of 8-16 weeks of age. You should be socializing your puppy throughout that time—it's not good enough to get some socialization in before the 'deadline' of 16 weeks!

Note: Cues for behaviors are capitalized throughout the text, as in Sit, Down, and Go To Your Bed. Book titles and important points are *italicized* and many important terms are in **bold** the first time they are used. To avoid the awkward he/she references, I have swapped back and forth between the pronouns he and she.

One more note: I recommend that you read at least the first two chapters before digging into the rest of the book. Once you have those chapters, the rest of the book will make more sense. I put the description of how to add a verbal cue or hand signal at the very end of this book because it's important to get the behavior before you start naming it. Even if you're just reading the book to learn how to teach Sit, please read the section on Adding a Cue before you set this book down for good. Thanks and happy reading! ☺

1

Communication & Learning Go Both Ways

Science is simply common sense at its best.
—Thomas Huxley

When you start to train your dog, you might be just trying to teach your dog to listen to you, but good training is more than simply teaching your dog to pay attention, it's also about paying attention to your dog's needs, what makes her stressed, and when she is having trouble understanding what you want her to do. Your dog is already paying attention to everything around her, including you. Learning about body language will help you understand your dog and allow you to communicate more clearly with your own body language. After we discuss the natural communication between you and your dog, we will explain how your dog learns to do what you want, using the science of learning.

Understanding Your Dog's Communication

I'm sure that one major reason that you are reading this book is to learn how to teach your dog to pay attention and respond to you in a reliable way. I could start the book with that, but there's a foundation that I'd like to lay down before you begin trying to influence your dog's behavior. I'd first like you to look at what your dog's ears, eyes, tail, and other body parts are doing and learn to interpret those movements as body language with meaning. Your training will go a lot more smoothly if you can understand more about what your dog is saying to you along the way.

First, let's talk about your dog's tail. Contrary to popular belief, *a wagging tail does not necessarily mean that your dog is happy*. A wagging tail means that a dog is excited, that there is adrenaline coursing through the dog's veins. A wagging tail goes with both happy and unhappy emotions. The good news is that you can usually interpret what's going on using the type of wag, the height of the tail, and the rest of the dog's body language. For example, if the wag extends through the whole body, so that the dog's hind end is wagging back and forth, that's a pretty good sign. If the body is stiff and the tail is wagging, that's usually a bad sign, i.e., the dog is basically saying "back off." The dog's tail is part of the spine and the tighter the muscles in the back, around spine, the higher the tail goes. Tight muscles are a sign of stress or conflict.

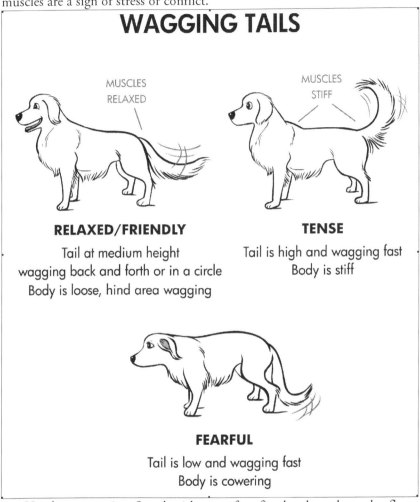

WAGGING TAILS

MUSCLES RELAXED

MUSCLES STIFF

RELAXED/FRIENDLY
Tail at medium height
wagging back and forth or in a circle
Body is loose, hind area wagging

TENSE
Tail is high and wagging fast
Body is stiff

FEARFUL
Tail is low and wagging fast
Body is cowering

Here's an exercise. Stand with your feet firmly planted on the floor. Imagine that someone has threatened your children. Take in a deep breath that makes your chest puff out. What happens to your tailbone? Your spine arches a little and your tailbone moves out. If you had a tail, it would've just gotten higher. Now imagine that you were a timid person and someone was about to strike you. Turn your head and crouch to avoid the blow. Your tailbone tucks, doesn't it? It's the same for dogs. A tail that is high in a flag is a sign that the dog is on the verge of fighting. A tucked tail is a sign of fear and such a dog may also fight if she is cornered. Now imagine that you've just won the lottery and do a happy dance. Really, do it right now if you can do so without looking goofy. What happens to your spine? Your spine is loose and your whole body wiggles. That's joy!

Calm, Happy Dog: Loose joints, soft or wiggly body, ears at middle/neutral position, dog moving at a 'normal' dog pace, 'soft' eyes looking at you but not staring hard, tail wagging in a circle at a moderate pace, relaxed down, sleeping, leaning into petting, taking treats easily without snatching, mouth soft and open, breath rate or panting matches the temperature and level of exercise the dog is doing, dog walks in curved lines and body is slightly curved when approaching other dogs or people. The black dog here, Peanut, was showing calm attention to me while I took his picture on a camping trip. In the photo, his mouth is open, he is looking at me, his  ears are mid-height for him, the pupils are not overly dilated (reflective), he is sitting on cue. The muscles in his face are standing out a tiny bit, but that matches the level of exercise.

Signs of Stress or Conflict: During your training sessions, you should notice that your dog is having a good time, rather than showing the signs of stress that follow. If you do see signs of stress, take a break and think about what aspect of your training is causing stress. Maybe you are accidentally using punishment when you really should be using reinforcement, maybe your body language is causing stress, or perhaps you are asking too much for your dog's skill level.

- Tight muscles
- Yawning
- Ears pinned back like the boxer shown here, ("let me get away")
- Ears tipped forward ("I really need that ball" or "I'm going to get that guy before he gets me")
- Sniffing around distractedly ("this training is confusing and stressful")
- Dog walking in slow motion
- Dry panting that doesn't match the temperature
- Scanning for danger—head turning quickly to look in all directions at once

- Suddenly moving faster during wrestling (arousal level increasing)
- Turning away to avoid touch ("let me get away")
- Tongue flicking out quickly like the boxer in the picture ("I'm a bit uncomfortable")
- Snatching treats quickly ("I'm only still here because I like the treats")
- No appetite for treats ("I'm so stressed that I can't even eat")
- Tail high in a flag ("go away")
- Tail tucked ("let me get away")
- Body crouched down ("let me get away")
- Body extra tall and squarely facing something ("go away")
- Dog avoids you or instantly rolls on his back when you approach or reach for him ("please don't attack me")
- Urination during greeting ("please don't attack me")
- Stink-eye—head turned away but eyes staring at you or another animal ("this is mine!")
- Stiff/freezing (especially with a hard stare)
- Barking
- Baring teeth
- Growling
- Biting

How can you use your understanding of these behaviors? Watch your own dog interact with other people and dogs to see what is 'normal' for your dog and which body postures are signs of stress. A tucked tail for a curved-tail dog (Shiba Inu, Pug, Husky, etc.) looks like a neutral tail for a Golden Retriever. The height of a happy tail for an Italian Greyhound can look like a tucked tail for a German Shepherd. Watching your dog's body when he meets others can be a powerful learning experience! How does his body change when he sees squirrels? When she meets the neighbor's dog? When he meets your niece? When your partner pets her on the head? When you pet him on the side or chest? Use this information about your dog's stress level to guide how you interact with your dog.

SIGNS OF STRESS

These behaviors can signal that your dog is scared,
depending on the context. Hire a trainer if they are extreme.

YAWNING

TONGUE FLICKS

DRY PANTING

STOPPING TO SNIFF

REFUSING TO
GO FORWARD

DELIBERATELY IGNORING
SOMETHING/SOMEONE

Lili Chin image, reprinted from "Behavior Adjustment Training" by Grisha Stewart

CROUCHED, SHIVERING,
WORRIED FACE

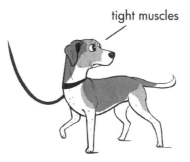

tight muscles

UNABLE TO
LOOK AWAY

SWEATY FEET,
DANDRUFF & SHEDDING

FLEEING/PULLING HOME

SCANNING AROUND
FOR DANGER

BARKING, GROWLING,
LUNGING, BITING

Learning Theory

So far, your dog has tried to read your intentions by watching what you do when you are around her. Now that you know more about body language, you can use your body's movements to communicate intentionally with your dog, but the words that come out of your mouth may not have any meaning. That's where a simple application of the science of learning comes in. My goal with this section is to give you a big picture description of how dogs learn. We'll get into the details of each behavior in the chapters that follow, but knowing how your dog may have learned to do what he's currently doing may help convince you that he's not stubborn or stupid. He's just responding to the consequences that have come from you and the rest of his environment. So he's already trained—just not in the way you want him to be.

At Ahimsa, we use the scientific principles of learning theory as the model training. That may sound technical, but it's not. The basic idea of the theory is that *dogs only do what works for them*. By this I mean that normal animals, including *dogs and humans, repeat behaviors that are followed by reinforcement and decrease behaviors that result in punishment*. It's like survival of the fittest for behaviors, based on the consequences that each behavior brings. All behaviors that contribute to the dog's survival and happiness survive and other behaviors go extinct.

Both reinforcement and punishment can involve either giving things to the dog or taking them away, so that gives us a total of four types of consequences for changing behavior. There's a wide ethical gap between those different consequence categories because of the stress that they cause. If you remember the basic idea that your dog's behaviors are a result of consequences, you're ahead of the game. Let's look at the four ways that consequences can affect behavior.

- Four types of consequences for behavior

Let's break that down. If a dog does something, like bark, you can follow it up with four different types of consequences. I like to think of them in terms of the emotion they cause. Brain research is showing us that dogs do have emotions, even if they may not be experienced with the same level of consciousness. *Behavior is reinforced by feelings of joy or relief. Behavior is punished by causing a feeling of discomfort or loss.* If a dog barks and he feels joy or relief, he's likely to bark in a similar situation in the future. If he barks and feels discomfort or loss, he's less likely to bark again in a similar situation. Let's look at this in more technical terms.

You can use reinforcers (stuff dogs want, ☺) or aversives (stuff dogs avoid, ☹) to train, but they don't have the same effect, even though this chart makes them look equal. If you're using artificial aversives (☹) on your dog, like choke chains, electronic collars, etc., stop now! It's better late than never. Life's too short to add more pain, especially when you can train your dog and solve problems without it! There can be unpredictable side effects of using force-based methods, like an increase in aggression.

Instead of using artificial aversives (☹) to train, I use the intelligence and creativity that makes humans 'superior' to set a dog up for success, so that I can reward with things the dog wants (☺). That means *I set up the situation so that doing what I want is the obvious choice for the dog.* I rarely use any kind of punishment, even time outs (negative punishment), but especially avoid corrections involving pain, fear or discomfort (positive punishment).

	(give) positive	(remove) negative
reinforcement	☺	☹
punishment	☹	☺

☺ = stuff dogs work to get
☹ = stuff dogs work to avoid

With my own dog, something like "ack" pops out of my mouth on rare occasions. That said, I know it's not particularly helpful to just shout at the dog, but I'm a verbal human being, and it just happens. When I do say "ack," I go through the situation again in my head to see if there was a way to handle the situation without resorting to sounding like a cave dweller. *Any time you find yourself wanting to use punishment, your job is to change the situation so that you can use reinforcement instead.* That's the intelligent way to be a "leader," rather than using brute force. We'll talk more about that in the chapter on problem solving, "Getting Rid of Problem Behaviors."

- **Reinforcement** is anything that increases motivation to do a particular behavior, i.e., makes that behavior stronger/more likely in the future.
- **Punishment** is anything that decreases motivation to do a behavior, i.e., makes a behavior weaker/less likely.

- The **Positive** column means that the dog is getting something, either something they want to happen or something they don't want to happen.
- The **Negative** column means something is taken away from the dog. They can be relieved or unhappy about that. Think subtraction or take-away.

Here are the four ways to reward and punish behavior:

- **Positive Reinforcement** (seeking JOY, PLEASURE). The dog gets something they like and that makes them more likely to repeat whatever they just did. If they sit and get a cookie, they are more likely to sit again. *Positive reinforcement is our primary method of training.*
- **Negative Reinforcement** (seeking RELIEF). Something the dog was unhappy or stressed about went away when she did a certain behavior, so that behavior is more likely to be repeated. An example of what I might do is notice that in a greeting, a puppy turns her head away from me, so I stop petting her (see info on BAT in the section on fear and aggression) to reward her head turn and honor her request for relief of social pressure. An example of what I would NOT do is to shock or "buzz" a dog with an electronic collar until she sat down. Sitting would still be rewarded, but I would not consider that to be humane training.
- **Negative Punishment** (avoiding SADNESS, LOSS). Something the dog wanted went away when she did a certain behavior, so she's less likely to repeat it next time. For example, your dog jumps up for attention and you leave the room for 15 seconds. Jumping up led to her not getting what she wanted, so it's less likely to happen again.
- **Positive Punishment** (avoiding DISCOMFORT, AVERSION, FEAR). Something unpleasant happened to the dog when she did a certain behavior, so she's less likely to repeat it next time. For example, in old-school training, if your dog jumped up, you would jerk on her leash. Jumping up led to her feeling pain, so it's less likely to happen again. She's also more likely to be stressed, so I avoid it. Corrections, such as jerking on the leash, "stim" (aka electric shock), kicking the dog, squirting with water, and pinning the dog down to achieve "calm submission" are all in this category. Shaking your finger at the dog or saying "tsst" are only in this category if doing those things actually punish the dog's behavior—

many dogs don't seem to change their behavior permanently when scolded this way, although it sometimes stops the behavior in the moment or gets your finger bitten. For some dogs, that kind of attention is actually reinforcing!

> **NOTE!**
> B.F. Skinner, father of the science of behaviorism, found that *punishment is not effective in the long run* because punished behaviors don't go away completely. You need to *reinforce something else* that you want the dog to do. For any problem behavior, there is a replacement behavior that you can reward.

- Focus on the good stuff

By controlling the food, toys, and opportunities that the dog likes, I control the dog's behavior. There's no need to shout, squirt the dog, shake her by the scruff, alpha roll her, or do anything else that doesn't fit my view

of how intelligent beings should treat one another. *Since we have the option of training any dog to do anything without force, there's no reason to use barbaric, outdated methods*.

Punishment usually goes hand-in-hand with the outdated dominance theory, which urges people to get the upper hand on their dogs by doing things that range from the benign (eating before the dog) to the inconvenient (walking through all doorways first) to the dangerous (pinning the dog to the ground or lifting the dog in the air by his collar to cut off the airway). At Ahimsa Dog Training, we count on the science of animal behavior and don't need to resort to outdated methods involving force. That frees us up to do things like teach dogs to do cool tricks, like lying down on a person's back (see the photo), which might be considered worrisome "domination" in old-school training.

Decades ago, science moved us beyond the need for dominance-based methods to help fix problems we have with our dogs. For example, the American Veterinary Society for Animal Behavior urges veterinarians to avoid recommending trainers who use dominance-based methods. Unfortunately, old-school methods have gained traction again due to popular television shows, but fortunately, people are starting to take off the rose-colored glasses and recognize that kind of training as abuse. If you still enjoy dog training TV shows that use choke chains, take a look at the color of the dog's tongue when the trainer lifts the dog into the air by the collar to put the dog into a 'submissive' state. The dog's tongue can actually turn blue that way, so that's not submission—the dog is just passing out. Another way to see what's really going on is to turn off the sound and watch the show in terms of the stress/happiness behaviors that I mentioned at the beginning of the book.

If a dog trainer, behaviorist, veterinarian, or friend suggests any techniques that make you uncomfortable, don't do that training with your dog. *You are your dog's advocate*. As the human, training decisions are ultimately up to you and rest entirely upon your own conscience.

If you have already done that kind of training, don't worry. You can still teach your dog using the techniques in this book. Your dog will love the change! If your dog could talk, he would probably quickly forgive your training methods used in the past and thank you for being open to learning about force-free training.

- Killing with kindness: a note on rewards

Rewards are something that we give or do to dogs in an attempt to reinforce behavior, but a reward only works if the dog actually finds it reinforcing! For example, petting will only reinforce behavior if your dog enjoys being petted at that moment. A surprising number of dogs really don't like being petted in the way that people pet them, and there are usually times where dogs don't want any petting at all. It's kind of like having your mom hug you when dropping you off for high school—in front of that cute guy you have a crush on.

If your dog doesn't like petting, you may actually be punishing her for being good! Here are some ways you can know the difference between petting and pestering.

If you reach for your dog and she pulls away, it's not petting. It's pestering! Petting is not reinforcing at that moment.

- Use the **5-second rule for petting**. Don't pet for more than 5 seconds at a time. After at most 5 seconds of petting, pull your hands away and see what your dog does. If she nuzzles your hand or looks at you, she probably enjoyed the petting. If she holds in one place or turns/moves away, you were pestering her.
- If a dog flips over on her back, as if to get a belly rub, she may not actually want that. She may just be afraid of you. If it's not your dog, assume that the dog doesn't actually want a belly rub.

With your own dog, instead of the 5-second rule, use something more like the 1-second rule, i.e., stop after just barely petting. In the belly rub session seen in the photo on the previous page, I stopped every second or so to make sure the dog, James, was still enjoying it. My dog, Peanut, actually prefers for me to massage his back when he goes into 'belly rub position.' I just put my hand between him and the floor or bed, palm up, and move along his back, massaging the muscles on the sides of his spine. Think about it, which part of you really needs a massage, your back or your belly?

If you want to make it more likely that your dog will enjoy petting from you, use wiggly fingers, i.e., massage versus patting him. Make contact with the part of the dog that is closest to you, rather than reaching over his body to touch something farther away. Crouch down and turn sideways to the dog, rather than leaning over.

Toys and treats are excellent ways to motivate your dog. It's important to not use them as a 'bribe,' but rather to have them be a surprise. In other words, when you use treats or toys, try to have them not be obvious to the dog until after he's done what you ask. For example, have the treats in your hand behind your back, in your pocket, in a treat pouch, or better yet, take the treats off of your body at least some of time, like up on a shelf or hidden in a tree. Try to surprise the dog with the reward after he sits or does whatever you've asked him to do.

You'll learn more about how to use treats effectively in a bit. Let's talk about which treats or toys you can actually use with your dog.

Basically, anything that is healthy to the dog can be used as a treat. You can even use some unhealthy things, but try not to give your dog too many of them. Look for natural and organic ingredients with names that you can recognize. Avoid foods that contain corn, sugar, ingredients sourced in countries with low standards for processing food, and anything with the words 'animal,' 'by-product', or 'digest.' While we're on the subject of health, watch your dog's weight, too. Your dog should have a waist if you look at him from above, and you should be able to feel your dog's ribs easily through the fur. If not, you need to either exercise your dog more, use lower calorie treats, use regular dog food as treats, feed less dog food overall, or all of the above.

Consider more than just the health factor for treats. *Your dog will love the behaviors only as much as she loves the training treats you used*, so don't just use your regular ho hum dog food. Get treats and have your dog sample them and rate them from low to WOW.

Treat Examples:
- Dog food (kibble)
- Cheese
- Veggie hot dogs
- Freeze dried lamb lung
- Salmon strips
- Chicken
- Tug toys
- Fetch toys
- Ice cubes
- Freeze-dried or fresh veggies
- Paper towel rolls
- Food puzzles

Dogs Learn Through Experience: Puppy Socialization

Teaching your dog doesn't just involve telling her what you want her to do, and vice versa. It is also about teaching your dog that she lives in a world that is safe and predictable, and how to cope with it when it is neither of those things. If you have a puppy, socialization should be your main focus in the weeks and months to come. *Puppy socialization is low-stress exposure to various aspects of everyday life*—people, dogs, surfaces, noises, etc. As author and trainer Pat Miller has said, "The idea of puppy socialization is to *give the dog a generally optimistic view of the world*" (my emphasis).

Why should you care? For one thing, puppies who are not well-socialized often have problems with aggression or manners later in life. Un- and under-socialized dogs are not comfortable with the world they live in and are less able to cope with change than they should be. Many dogs at the shelter that look abused were actually just under-socialized as puppies.

People are often afraid of the germs that their puppy might encounter when they are out in the world, but *the major killer of dogs in the U.S. is not disease, it's behavior, which is directly correlated to puppy socialization*. For most of the dogs, that could have been changed with early socialization and puppy training.

Because of our current understanding of the importance of behavior, and because of vaccine advancements, we can start socializing puppies earlier than we used to do. Most of the new puppy vaccines can be given starting at 6 weeks old, and start being effective for relatively clean environments about 10 days later. Previous vaccines would fight with the immunization given by the mother and thus lose effectiveness, but newer vaccines have solved this problem, so we can vaccinate earlier than we could years ago. After your puppy gets his first round of shots, he is ready to be carefully exposed to the world. We still need to minimize risks for disease until the vaccinations are complete (usually 3 sets of combo shots) and keep the socialization fun for your puppy. That's the key to everything – socialization is a fun experience for your puppy.

If your veterinarian disagrees, you can tell her/him that the American Veterinary Society of Animal Behavior recommends starting puppy classes 7 days after your puppy's first set of shots, in most cases. You can see their position paper online at http://avsabonline.org/resources/position-statements (also includes positions on dominance, how to choose a trainer, and more).

Make sure that the school that you take your puppy to keeps medical and emotional risks to a minimum. For example, at Ahimsa, we have the facility professionally cleaned with a virucide the night before each puppy class, ask all puppy owners for proof of vaccination, and ask our students to avoid the dog park while they are in puppy class. We also have a special class for younger puppies, called Baby Puppy, so younger puppies do not have to start out in the main kindergarten class. If your training school doesn't have that option, the instructor should be doing something to make sure younger puppies are not bullied by older puppies. For example, young puppies can watch play time from behind a barrier at first.

Your puppy is learning and socializing right now, during every second that he's awake. People used to say that you couldn't start obedience training with a puppy until it was six months old. But they meant you couldn't properly punish a dog until that age with a choke chain, because of their growing puppy bones. *With positive training methods, you don't have to wait to begin training.* Using positive training, some dog breeders send home puppies that already know how to sit on cue. That's just one more reason to be dog-friendly—you can teach your puppy manners now! You can and should start teaching your puppy basic cues, like sit, down, etc. using the techniques in this book. But your main focus during puppyhood should not be on 'obedience' type behaviors, but rather on socialization with other puppies, dogs, humans, surfaces, sounds, and more, as well as everyday manners within your home.

Puppies are socialization sponges. Things that they experience in this time period will stick with them forever. Sources differ, but many say that the primary socialization period is up until 12 weeks. From 12-16 weeks, they are learning as well, but not as quickly as they did up to 12 weeks. Every new experience for your puppy should be positive, i.e., accompanied by treats, praise, and/or fun. Up until 6 months, you should only have your puppy in socializing environments that you have solid control over. Even after that, your puppy is still socializing. You may be surprised to learn that the full socialization period for a puppy is two years! But your dog will be your companion for 10 to 15 more years, so why not invest some time into creating an optimistic dog now?

To what sort of things should you socialize your new puppy? Everything!! Your puppy should experience a bit of cold, funny noises, strange hats, interesting textures, calm restraint (praise and release it when it is calm), other dogs (your own dogs are not enough!) and many other things. Puppies should also learn to stop mouthing, gradually (see the section below on puppy biting). All of these topics in a good puppy socialization class, but you should start with exposing your puppy to new things now. Socialization doesn't just mean play with dogs. You can search online for "Puppy's Rule of Twelve" to find an article by Margaret Hughes with a variety of ideas.

Dog-dog interactions should be controlled and positive for your dog. You can socialize your young puppy with dogs in a positive puppy training class, a puppy playgroup, or a neighbor's yard, but not the dog park! One recent study found that dogs about 6 month of age were the target for the most aggression in the park, more than any other age group. Once your dog is old enough to go to the dog park, and you decide it's worth the risk, protect him from harm by moving along and not letting him get harassed by other dogs. If you have a small-breed dog, you should probably wait even longer than six months before going to the dog park, if ever. There are opportunities for play and socialization outside of the park, and you should take advantage of them.

Your dog is still 'socializing' even if she is not doing rough-and-tumble play, so going on walks with friends and meeting older dogs who do not play will still be very useful. Shy dogs can gain confidence around dogs who aren't trying to get them to play and dogs who tend to get overly riled up will learn manners around dogs who immediately going into play mode.

Again, make sure all experiences are safe and generally positive for your puppy. Your puppy should be able to leave or stop an interaction whenever he wants. Slow down and add distance if your puppy is scared! Please *read through the information on BAT and counterconditioning in this book,* even if your puppy has not shown any fears. Both techniques are helpful for socialization.

Now let's start talking about some of the technicalities of training. In our puppy socialization classes and adult dog classes, we use clicker training. What is it, exactly? Read on!

2

Clicker Training Works!

I was skeptical about the effectiveness of clicker training before my first session with Grisha, but by the end of our first class I had no doubts. Our dog Indy loves his training sessions, and is always excited when he sees us bring out the clicker. He has a focus and desire to get down to work that I didn't expect from a puppy. We absolutely believe in the methods Grisha uses, and have been delighted to find that our dog can and will learn without resorting to punitive measures.
—Chris M., Ahimsa client in Seattle

What is a Clicker?

Clicker training is about using a signal to pinpoint and highlight correct behavior choices. Clicker training doesn't actually require any gadgets, but we often use a clicker to maximize the effectiveness of clicker training. A clicker is a small box that makes a noise. The sound of the click is like praise, but stronger. It is used to teach new behaviors to animals of many different species, including humans (see TagTeach.com). For a dog, a click is always paired with a reward—a click is a promise to the dog that he is about to get a treat. It is not for getting his attention, but *for telling him that he has done something that you'd like to see repeated.*

Think of a clicker as a camera that takes pictures of good behaviors, increasing the chance that you'll see the good behavior again. (Sort of like that childhood taunt, "Take a picture, it lasts longer!") I have used clicker training to train a goat, some cats, my wife, and myself, but let's talk about the clicker as it is used with dogs.

Some dogs are afraid of the sound of the clicker or are deaf. For these dogs and for any time you want to train quietly, you can use a different marker.

A marker is a signal that tells your dog his behavior has just earned a reward, exactly as the clicker would. I often use a verbal marker (like Yes!) or a visual marker (like a hand flash—your hand goes quickly from fist to five to fist in front of the dog).

Clicker trainers first teach the dog the behavior and then put it on cue, so the dog does the behavior when asked. *Focusing on success and teaching the behavior before the cue is a very important difference from old-fashioned training!*

Once your dog knows what you're looking for, and he knows what you call that behavior ("sit," for example), you can stop using the clicker and either switch to a verbal marker or no marker at all. That means that you won't need to carry the clicker around with you forever. ☺

Let me repeat that—**you won't need to carry the clicker around forever.** It's not a tool that causes or triggers behavior. It just rewards good choices in a really effective way.

Why Does the Clicker Work?

- The sound is sharp and distinct, something the dog doesn't hear elsewhere.

- The clicker is fast and accurately marks the moment.

- The clicker is the same sound no matter who in your family is using it.

You can use clicker training to teach any animal that eats (that would be all of them) to do anything that he is physically capable of doing—from leg weaves (shown here) to calm relaxation to heeling. Once you start teaching using clicker training, the speed of learning seems to snowball, and your dog will pick up new behaviors more and more quickly. Behaviors taught with progressive reward-based training should also be reliable and durable, meaning your dog will be able to respond quickly, the first time you ask for a behavior, and remember their training for a really long time. If you add in the fact that the dogs and people seem to be having such a fun time, why do it any other way?

Later in this book, you will learn all about how to use the clicker to teach your dog new behaviors. But first, let's get to what most of you are here for, how to get your dog to STOP doing something that she is already doing.

3

Getting Rid of Problem Behaviors

No problem can stand the assault of sustained thinking.
—Voltaire

From our short lesson on Learning Theory, you know that dogs only repeat behaviors if there is some form of reinforcement. We don't always provide that reinforcement on purpose. Sometimes the environment reinforces the dog's behaviors. Chasing a cat is very rewarding, but we did not provide that. Sometimes we reinforce the dog on accident, like when we allow them to pull forward on a tight leash.

The two main ways that we will get rid of problem behavior are to **remove rewards for problem behavior** and to **give the dog something to DO instead**.

Jumping & Other Accidentally Trained Behaviors

Cute Puppy Fido is allowed to jump up and get lots of petting. That's a huge reinforcement history to overcome when the family finally decides that Giant Adolescent Fido needs to stop jumping. Even pushing Fido off reinforces the behavior, because sparring with paws is one of the ways dogs greet each other.

Remove rewards for problem behavior: This is the management side of dog training. If the dog is chewing the garbage, remove or cover the garbage. If he is chewing your shoes, put the shoes up and/or crate him while you can't watch him. If he is jumping on you when you come home, don't look at him or pay attention to him in any way (even to say "off" or "no") until he's on the ground.

If your dog is jumping up on people during your walks, step on the leash before you let Fido be greeted or put a treat to his nose to lure him past the distraction, so that he doesn't lunge at the distraction on the way past. If he's jumping on guests at home, tether him to a couch or the wall, having your guest approach him when he is on the ground and back away when he's jumping. If he's chasing the cat, keep Fido and the cat in separate rooms when you're not around. If he pulls like a maniac to greet another dog, do NOT let him drag you over there. Think how reinforcing greeting his own species will be to your dog! Use that as a reward for good behavior instead.

If your dog is doing something you don't want him to do, like jumping up, have your family sit down and write out the ways that Fido is being reinforced for this behavior. Next, come up with ways to keep him from getting reinforced. Finally, work up a list of what you want him to do instead.

You may actually want your dog to jump up at certain times. Say you have a small dog like the Bichon Frise in the photo here, and you want to allow jumping up when you are seated (or even all the time). In that case, be really clear with your dog about when jumping is allowed. The default should be that the dog gets no attention for jumping up unless you have invited the dog to jump.

For example, you could have a cue, like Kisses, for times when your dog is allowed to jump up and kiss your face. At other times, you would simply stand up or turn away. Note: Small dogs will often jump up on you in times that they are afraid. If that is the case, you can either do something to make the situation less scary (my preference) or pick them up. It's better to reward jumping up than to teach them that they have no help in a scary world, so that they must defend themselves with growling and snarling.

Give your dog something to DO: So far, we have removed rewards for behavior we don't like, but the dog still has a need. If you don't find something different for Fido to do in the situations that he misbehaves, he'll come up with something on his own to get his needs met. Chances are, you won't like his new behavior choices either. You can avoid this problem by picking a behavior you like and rewarding him with real-life rewards. When he greets you at the door, reward him with attention and treats for sitting, having all four paws on the ground (sticky paws), or going to get a toy. It's best to reward only sits or sticky paws that don't immediately follow a jump-up, or else the dog may make a **behavior chain**, like jump-then-sit. A behavior chain is two or more behaviors linked together, where the last behavior gets a reward and thus all of the behaviors in the chain are reinforced. When you are reinforcing the sit or other good choices that don't involve jumping, the reward can be food or attention— just make sure that the attention goes away again if the dog returns to jumping.

Reward him for taking a toy instead of chasing the cat. Reward him for looking at you or targeting your finger while out on walks, rather than jumping up at strangers or other dogs.

Housetraining

Housetraining is another one of those issues where you want to prevent rehearsal of the 'bad' behavior and reward a replacement that you like better. We don't like it when they use our carpet as a toilet, but we love it when they go outside.

1. Prevent accidents indoors by keeping your dog in one of four states:
   a. **In a place where they can eliminate whenever they want**, like outside in your yard (with supervision). In the house, you can use a small area with a puppy pad if you're going to be gone for a really long time, but try to avoid situations where those are needed because you don't want

them rehearsing the use of your kitchen as a toilet area. Dog walkers can help with that.

b. **In a place where they 'cannot' eliminate**, like in a crate. They are unlikely to soil their crate. If they do, then clean it out and turn the crate into a big dog dish for a week or so, spreading kibble around in it. A general rule of thumb for young dogs is that puppies can be crated for their age in months, plus one. So a 3-month-old puppy could stay for only 4 hours without a break. Of course, your 1-year-old dog can't be crated for 13 hours, so use good judgment!

c. **Being watched like a hawk**, especially after mealtimes, play, drinking, and waking up. Tethering the puppy to you helps this process.

d. **Empty**—they've just gone pee and poo however many times they need to before they are empty. Puppies are only empty for about half an hour. Keep in mind you still need to watch out for destructive chewing!

2. Teach your dog to eliminate on cue. A few seconds before your puppy squats or lifts a leg to eliminate, calmly say your cue once. Just  once! Click and treat right as she finishes. For the cues, I use "be quick" for peeing and "hurry" for poo. I like to have words I can say in public that don't sound like I'm talking to a toddler! Go outside with the dog and treat right after the click!

3. Teach your dog to ring a bell to ask to go outside (optional). See the touch/targeting section for ideas.

If you're really having trouble with housetraining, first check your puppy's daily schedule to make sure she is being set up for success. You can do this yourself or have a force-free dog trainer come look at your home and talk through your training plan. If that all looks good, have your vet check health issues—a urinary tract infection or issues that cause excessive drinking will also cause housetraining trouble.

Puppy Biting & Chewing

Is your puppy nipping at you? Chewing on your furniture? It would actually be a bit odd if your puppy wasn't biting and chewing. Puppies explore the world with their teeth and spend a good deal of their time in the litter mouthing each other. Your job is to teach the puppy what is appropriate to put her teeth on (toys, other dogs) and what is not (furniture, people). A good puppy socialization class will go a long way in helping with the biting.

If your puppy chews on furniture, carpets, or the kids' toys, fall back on the problem solving strategy mentioned above. First, *remove the reward* by either not having the chewing item available (e.g., kids put their toys away or there is a baby gate blocking the dog from the kids' toys) or by having the item taste yucky. To make the item taste bad, apply a bitter-tasting product, such as Bitter Apple spray, on the item that the dog was chewing. Don't spray the puppy! I don't recommend applying bitter products to kids' toys, but it is great for furniture. Spray in a spot where it's not likely to be seen, at first, in case there is damage to the material. Refresh the bitter spray daily until your puppy gives up chewing in that area. Second, *give the puppy something to do* by providing toys that are similar to what she wants to chew on. You may need to remind her that the toys are there. If she starts to ponder chewing on your couch, distract her and get her interested in chewing on a toy that is a similar texture. While she's chewing the toy, spray the couch leg with Bitter Apple.

Focus on teaching her how to interact with you in a way that doesn't use her teeth. When you pet or groom her, click and treat for good interactions like nuzzling, licking, choosing not to bite. Be really fast and catch every little small choice to not bite you. Biting is tempting for a puppy, so you'll need to be observant. On the other hand, if your puppy starts to bite, freeze and stop interacting for a little bit, like 10-15 seconds. Before you get started, you may want to set-up your getaway strategy. It may be that you do this exercise sitting on the floor with her and all you have to do is stand up and she'll notice that you're gone. But some puppies just start biting even more at that point. In that case, one idea is to get set up in a puppy-proof room that you can quickly leave from by stepping over a baby gate or shutting a door behind you. Another way is to have the puppy in a harness and attach her leash to the couch or a door handle. Then all you have to do is move out of range.

In your everyday life, you may have to have your puppy drag a short leash so it's easy to put him into another room to settle down, without a lot manhandling. Manhandling can be interpreted as fun play for your puppy, and you don't want to accidentally reward the biting by playing when he bites. Safety tip: never, ever leave a puppy tethered or dragging a leash without supervision.

It may take some creativity to figure out how to keep the puppy's biting from being reinforced, but your effort will pay off. The good news is that as long as your puppy's biting doesn't get reinforced with play or attention, the biting **will** go away. You don't need to resort to growling, pinning, or smacking your dog, which can make her afraid of people or more likely to find another target in your household. I've seen that exact situation several times. In every case, it was the husband who was able to control the dog through dominance-based methods and the others who suffered: the dog started biting the wife and children. Unfortunately, the fact that the dominance methods worked for the husbands made it hard to see that their behavior toward the dog was actually the cause of the issue for the other members of their family. The good news is that humans who are open to new information do learn, and when the husbands changed to positive reinforcement training, the dogs changed their behavior for the better, too. A side benefit was that the children had a chance to see the positive effects of treating a fellow being with respect and compassion. Knowing that violence begets violence, I imagine that paradigm shift improved not just their dog training, but also their human relationships.

15 Tips to Stop Barking in Class

Like puppy mouthiness, barking in class is extremely common; in fact just about all dogs will bark in class, given the chance. But some dogs bark more than others, and it can be hard to be the person with the barky dog in training class. Here is a list of some of the things that we've found to help with barking during class. You don't have to do all of them, but the more you do, the better chance you have of keeping your dog quiet. Gradually fade out these tools until your dog can work quietly in class without this added help.

1. Teach your dog a Focus Trick, like Spin or Touch (see directions later in this book for Touch). Whenever your dog begins staring at other dogs or looks generally antsy, you can cue a Focus Trick. Sometimes reward with praise and sometimes use treats or toys.

2. A good exercise session before class can help your barky dog calm down. A long walk with lots of sniffing and games where you hide treats or toys for the dog to find are better at settling most dogs down than a fast-paced game of fetch. Even if your dog is not barky, he may benefit from getting exercise right before class.

3. No food several hours before class. (For the dog, that is. You might want to eat if it helps you feel calm!)

4. Set up visual barriers between your dog and other dogs or distractions. Arriving to class before the other students will help you get set up in the best spot in your training classroom. Gradually open the curtains or move the barriers so that your dog is exposed to more and more of the room. This may happen in one session or over the course of several classes.

5. Busy dogs are quiet! Dogs will often stare at each other and then bark when the instructor is speaking to the class, because they're not getting as much attention from their humans. Interrupt your dog if he locks eyes with some other dog across the room. Kongs with peanut butter, bully sticks, and other food-based toys can make a big difference. Your class instructor may even have such toys available, but bring a variety of chew toys to distract your dog in class. Try to give her the toy before she starts barking. If she barks, get her attention back using her name or a tickle on her fur, ask for a sit, then give the toy. Tug toys may also work for some active tuggers, but that can get too loud sometimes, so be considerate of others when tugging during class.

6. Use the off switch. You can put your dog into a crate with her food puzzle during the lecture/demo parts of your class. If your dog is little, you might scoop him up to sit on your lap during those times. Calm, relaxed massage can help small and big dogs alike. As with the toys, try this approach before the barking starts.

7. There's a Dog Appeasing Pheromone collar that can keep them calm around town and in class. Many vets sell them.

8. "Doggie Calm" is aromatherapy that can help with barking. We sell that at the training center and online.

9. In class (and elsewhere), click and treat for calm behavior. The behavior to click is mostly attention to you, but catch all of those good decisions where he was thinking about barking, but doesn't. When you see him thinking of barking, which happens often when a new dog walks in the room, say his name or "shhhh" and click/treat for the one second of silence that produces. See Relaxation on Cue toward the end of this book.

10. Teach a cue to signal quiet time. This takes time, so you'll need to do the other things on this list in the meantime. Say "shhh" with your finger to your lips. When your dog is silent for one second, click and treat. Over time, start to require two, three, ten, or more seconds before clicking. At home, if the dog returns to barking, say "Too Bad!" and give her a brief time out in another room or a crate (if she's fine with her crate). After 30 seconds of silence, bring her back out. If you find that you are giving a lot of time outs, then you aren't rewarding the quiet times soon enough. Keep your expectations reasonable for your dog in that setting.

11. Bringing a rug for your dog to sit on can make him feel more at ease. Of course, that's what human laps are for if your dog fits. See Go To Your Bed at the end of this book.

12. Bring two people, so one person can work on keeping your dog quiet and the other can listen to the instructor.

13. If you're alone, learn to multi-task in class. Ask your dog for behaviors he already knows well, like lying down, targeting your hand, or tricks. Please use hand signals instead of words, though, or your voice will distract others, instead of your dog's barking!

14. If all else fails, you can put your dog in the car and come back to class to get the instruction. Work on "shhh" and attention to you for another week and your dog should be able to come back the next time!

15. Outside of class, train in situations where your attention is divided. Go sit on a park bench, bus stop, or coffee shop and practice the techniques listed above. You can also use the Frustrated Greeter exercises listen in the next section.

Fear, Frustration, and Aggression

Dogs are not small humans in furry suits, but they can still develop fear, happiness, and other emotions in response to the world around them, because those all come from the limbic system. The limbic system deals with survival and is also known as the mammalian brain in diagrams of the human brain. Sometimes fearful and aggressive behavior is actually a symptom of pain or some other a physical problem, so check with your veterinarian if something suddenly changes about your adult dog's temperament.

Puppies and adolescent dogs do have fear periods where they are suddenly more scared of everything, but that shouldn't happen in an adult dog. For puppies, the fear period is usually sometime between 8 and 11 weeks. An adolescent dog can have more than one fear period, sometime between 6 months and a year of age. If your young dog is suddenly afraid of more things, make sure the environment is as calm as possible for your puppy and expose him only very carefully to new things, using lots of fun and treats.

Different dogs have different 'Monsters.' My dog, Peanut, had many Monsters: children, people in hats, fireworks, and dogs that stare at or jump on him, to name a few. Dogs at any distance used to be Monsters, children were Monsters with a capital M, trashcans and nail trimmers were Monsters, and any people outside the family also were Monsters. My other dog loves people, including children, doesn't mind fireworks, but almost any dog over 20 pounds approaching her is a Monster. Generally, the ones who jump on her are immediately converted into playmates. The ones who sit back and watch, like Peanut, are her Monsters.

Dogs react differently to Monsters—Peanut shivered or barked from afar to scare the Monster off, while my other dog was likely to go in and do something to get the Monster to leave. Some dogs jump in the tub or hide under mom's legs, or show just a small tongue flick like the boxer shown at the beginning of the book. Whatever your dog does when she sees a Monster, one thing is for certain—it's not a good thing for physical or mental health. Animals (including humans) don't fare well under long-term stress.

Punishing your dog for barking, growling or lunging at a Scary Monster does not alleviate that stress; it just makes it worse. *Punishment simply takes away an outlet for your dog's stress and lulls you into thinking your dog is fine.* That's where bites without warning can come from—dogs have been corrected for growling, snarling, etc., so they don't. They hold on as long as they can, and then they snap.

Below I will explain two good methods for dealing with fear and aggression: Behavior Adjustment Training (BAT) and Classical Counterconditioning (CC). Both methods are paired with Systematic

Desensitization, which is a gradual approach for getting dogs used to things. I use BAT and CC in different situations or sometimes combine them. BAT can be used for frustration, too, which sometimes looks like aggression because of all of the barking and lunging. If you have a dog with fear or aggression issues, I'd also work on training Watch, U-turn (quickly turn toward you), Sit, walking nicely on leash, and Come. You can use those techniques to rehabilitate fear and aggression, but you can also use them to PREVENT issues, so even if you have a puppy with no fear issues, read on!

- Counterconditioning and systematic desensitization

One approach for fear and aggression to take is to work on the emotional side of things—to convince the dog the Monster is really not a Monster at all—in fact, it's a Very Good Thing. The way to do this is a very gradual process with many, many pairings of Monsters and Very Good Things. Here's some info on using counterconditioning and systematic desensitization to change your dog's opinion of Monsters:

Monsters ALWAYS cause Very Good Things. Pairing scary things with food or toys is called classical counterconditioning and the order is important. Let's say I want to convince you to enjoy the sound of a balloon being popped in your ear. That's the Monster. Say you love chocolate, but haven't had it in a long time (or never had it). That's your Very Good Thing. We'll forbid you from eating chocolate except in our experiment.

Let's say that I pop the balloon in the next room (so it wasn't too loud) and 1/4 of a second later gave you chocolate, then paused for a bit (with dogs I say about 1-2 minutes). If I then do that pairing again, balloon pop followed by chocolate 1/4 of a second later, then pause, then another pop/chocolate association, you'd start to see a connection. Then maybe the next day, we do some more pop/chocolate pairings, out of the blue. If we continue this and you never hear the balloon pop without receiving chocolate soon afterwards, you'd start to see it as very predictive. In fact, the researcher Ivan Pavlov would have noted that you'd start to salivate when you heard the pop (assuming we haven't given you so much chocolate that you're sick of it!). Over time, we could pop the balloon closer and closer to your head, each time following it with chocolate. You'd probably still startle a bit when you heard the pop, but your first response will be salivation and, "YAY, chocolate!" instead of, "Ack, who popped that?!"

That's the right way. Let's do another walk through with some of the mistakes people make. If you do the process backwards, as in Very Good Thing causes Monsters, the reverse would happen. I hand you chocolate, then pop a balloon. Randomly repeat, repeat, repeat. Soon, you start being tentative about taking the chocolate, because you're afraid of the balloon pop. No amount of telling yourself that the pop is a good thing will help. If you didn't much mind the pop in the first place, you might just start to not really notice the popping (you'll become 'desensitized'), but you might also just get even more annoyed or wary of the popping ('sensitized'). The same thing applies if the popping and the chocolate occur simultaneously.

The take-home message is that Monsters CAUSE Very Good Things. So the dog first sees the Monster, and then the Very Good Thing appears. Let's say a dog named Shy is afraid of other dogs, maybe even barks at other dogs. When Shy's ears perk up because she's seen another dog, the human instantly and joyously gives her a handful of turkey reserved just for this occasion, bite after bite, until the Monster dog is far enough away (usually something like 10 feet and moving away from you), then the fun stops as quickly as it started. Express your 'joy' at seeing the Monster in a happy, confident tone, one that you might use during play time. Don't scare your dog with your exuberance. Keep your leash loose but short.

ONLY Monsters cause Very Good Things. The value of the Very Good Thing and its connection to the Monster must be preserved, so only give the Very Good Thing in the presence of the Monster. Ideally, little Shy would never have even tasted turkey, or cheese, or wet cat food, or Natural Balance, or whatever Very Good Thing you're using, before giving it to her in the presence of other dogs. In mathematical lingo, Shy gets a Very Good Thing if, and only if, she's just seen a Monster.

Monsters must keep their DISTANCE. It's important to have the love of the Very Good Thing be stronger than the fear of the Monster. A child at 40 feet may not bother Rufus one bit, but a child at 20 feet may cause him to panic and start snarling and lunging. Very Good Things are quite strong distractions, but they're not foolproof. Don't expect cheese to calm Rufus when he's too close to the Monster. Rufus should see Monsters at whatever distance makes him "edgy." He should note the Monster, be a bit wary, but not scale an all-out defensive war or be so nervous that he can't eat. That may be something like 30 feet for Rufus. His ears perk up, he stiffens a bit, but doesn't start barking.

By starting at a distance that is very easy for the dog and gradually getting closer, we allow the dog to be comfortable all the way through. This is called Systematic Desensitization.

If your dog barks at the Scary Monster during this training, present the Very Good Thing anyway and move further away as quickly as you can. This may be slowed down by the fact that you're stuffing turkey into your dog's face! The same applies to noise sensitivity, but 'further away' probably means 'at a lower volume or intensity.' Because the dog barked last time, you may have to reduce the intensity to make the situation easier to handle.

Over the course of several trials, gradually move closer or in some way increase the intensity. Faster moving Monsters, louder Monsters, closer Monsters, more intense Monsters. The key word here is GRADUAL. This process should be like watching paint dry. Resist all urges to make things harder on Rufus before he's ready! That's one of the hardest parts of this whole process. Counterconditioning is especially useful for dogs who are uncomfortable with noises, being touched/groomed, or sharing their stuff.

COUNTERCONDITIONING & DESENSITIZATION
= Pairing Monsters with Very Good Things

1. Monsters ALWAYS cause Very Good Things
2. ONLY Monsters cause Very Good Things
3. Monsters must keep their DISTANCE, then, over many repetitions GRADUALLY get closer so that the dog is comfortable all the way through.

It is important to have the LOVE of the Very Good Things be stronger than the FEAR of the Monsters.

After many repetitions of...   You get...

- Behavior Adjustment Training (BAT)

BAT is a technique that I developed for my dog, Peanut, and ended up using with my other clients to reduce fear, aggression, and frustration. BAT gives dogs and other animals socially acceptable ways to communicate their needs. I made it while I rehabilitated my own dog, but now that people around the world are using it, BAT is helping a lot of dogs!

BAT is a systematic desensitization technique that uses functional and bonus rewards (I'll explain what that means) in an error-free approach to learning. This is the main technique that we use for dogs with social issues and fears of objects or places. BAT is used for barking at or attacking other dogs and people, chasing cars, fear of getting into the car, attacking the vacuum cleaner, fear and avoidance of people, and a lot of other issues. The dog pictured below used to be very aggressive toward livestock. His caretaker used  BAT to help him gain comfort and learn to control himself.

When your dog does something you don't like, the behavior is usually triggered by something that happens in her environment. Doing the behavior serves a function: it fulfills a need or want, so we say that the dog gets a **functional reward** for behavior triggered by the **environmental cue**.

Environmental Cue → Behavior → Functional Reward

The functional reward for behavior done after seeing a steak is the eating of the steak. The functional reward of behaviors done after spotting the squirrel is getting closer to / chasing the squirrel. Think of another behavior your dog does and try to pair it with a functional reward. If you have a partner or a child, you can apply this same sort of thinking to them, too. Think something that your partner or child does and think about what they get out of doing it, i.e., what is the functional reward?

FUNCTIONAL REWARDS

Doing a behavior fulfills a need or a want, so we say that the dog gets a Functional Reward for the behavior triggered by the environmental cue.

Environmental Cue → BEHAVIOR → Functional Reward

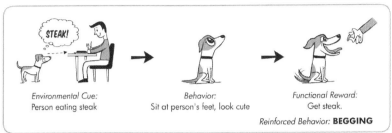

Environmental Cue:
Person eating steak

Behavior:
Sit at person's feet, look cute

Functional Reward:
Get steak.

Reinforced Behavior: **BEGGING**

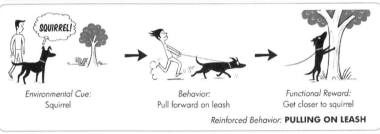

Environmental Cue:
Squirrel

Behavior:
Pull forward on leash

Functional Reward:
Get closer to squirrel

Reinforced Behavior: **PULLING ON LEASH**

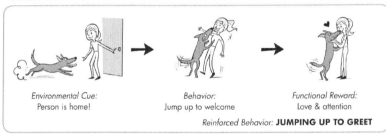

Environmental Cue:
Person is home!

Behavior:
Jump up to welcome

Functional Reward:
Love & attention

Reinforced Behavior: **JUMPING UP TO GREET**

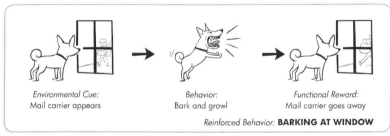

Environmental Cue:
Mail carrier appears

Behavior:
Bark and growl

Functional Reward:
Mail carrier goes away

Reinforced Behavior: **BARKING AT WINDOW**

REPLACEMENT BEHAVIORS

It is always good to think of a Replacement Behavior (or Alternate Behavior) - what you want your dog to do - and reinforce this behavior instead of thinking in terms of punishment. *The Functional Reward remains the same.

Environmental Cue → REPLACEMENT BEHAVIOR → Functional Reward

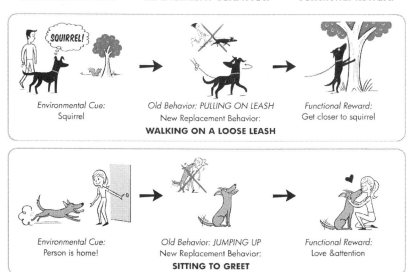

Environmental Cue: Squirrel	*Old Behavior: PULLING ON LEASH* New Replacement Behavior: **WALKING ON A LOOSE LEASH**	*Functional Reward:* Get closer to squirrel
Environmental Cue: Person is home!	*Old Behavior: JUMPING UP* New Replacement Behavior: **SITTING TO GREET**	*Functional Reward:* Love &attention

FUNCTIONAL REWARD TRAINING

1. Figure out the Functional Reward for the Problem Behavior
2. Reinforce the alternate behavior (when dog makes good choices)
3. Give access to the Functional reward - fulfill the need that triggered the behavior you are trying to change

To discover the functional reward of a **problem behavior** (something your dog is doing that you don't like), look at the consequence of the dog's behavior—what are they earning from the people, dogs, and world around them by doing the behavior? For example, when dogs show aggression, one big consequence is usually an increase in distance from the trigger (they scare it away or are allowed to leave themselves).

We can use an increased distance—i.e., walking away from the trigger—as a functional reward for some other kind of behavior that you want the dog to do instead. The new behavior (the one we want our dogs to do) is called a **replacement behavior**, or alternate behavior. It is always good to think in terms of what you want the dog to do, so you can reinforce that behavior instead of thinking in terms of punishment. Some good replacement behaviors include loosening her leash (replaces pulling), sitting (replaces jumping up), licking or softly muzzling (replaces biting), etc.

Here is one way to get rid of any problem behavior:

1. *Analyze the problem behavior* to find the functional reward. What does your dog get out of doing what he's doing?
2. Set up a Choice Point to *Expose* the dog to a subtle version of the situation that triggers the problem behavior. Don't make it so realistic that the dog does the problem behavior. Breathe calmly.
3. *Wait* for good choices, i.e. replacement behaviors that your dog can do instead of the problem behavior. If stress increases, stop the situation and start over in a better way instead of letting your dog flounder.
4. *Mark* the good choice with a word or clicker.
5. Give access to a *Functional Reward*—fulfill the need that triggered the behavior you are trying to change.
6. Give an optional *Bonus Reward*, like food or a toy.

When to use this kind of training:

1. You can figure out what the functional reward is for the problem behavior.
2. You can control access to the functional reward.
3. There is an alternate behavior that will reasonably earn the same functional reward in the dog's everyday life.

BAT is this kind of training applied to fear, aggression, and frustration. You can use BAT to help socialize puppies, too. Most dogs show aggressive behavior because they are either trying to chase something/someone away or to run away from the Scary Monster. In other words, the functional reward is an increase in distance to the trigger. The description of the three BAT Stages below applies to this kind of reactivity.

For some dogs, the functional reward is the opposite of walking away. Frustrated Greeters are dogs who bark, lunge, or whine to go closer, rather than further away. For Frustrated Greeters, follow the steps below, but use one step of forward progress as the reward each time the dog does a replacement behavior (head turn, ground sniff, etc.). If you have a puppy who is just starting to show fear or frustration, using BAT can prevent leash reactivity. See my "Give Your Puppy a Choice" DVD for a puppy demo.

BASIC BAT SET-UP

STEP 1: CHOICE POINT. Dog notices the trigger from a safe distance.

*Pick a distance where the dog is below threshold and not likely to overreact.

STEP 2: WAIT FOR A GOOD CHOICE. Prompt if you have to.

*Look for an ENGAGE- DISENGAGE pattern or a CUT-OFF SIGNAL

STEP 3: MARK the good choice at the precise moment.

* For example, use a verbal marker like "YES!" You may use a clicker only if you are using FOOD or TOYS as a Bonus Reward (STEP 5)

STEP 4: FUNCTIONAL REWARD = distance from the trigger.

*Walk or jog the dog away from the trigger on loose leash

STEP 5: (OPTIONAL) BONUS REWARD = Food or Toys

*The optional treat/toy comes AFTER the Functional Reward.

RINSE, REPEAT...

Lili Chin image, reprinted from "Behavior Adjustment Training" by Grisha Stewart

If Your Dog Goes Over Threshold

If the trigger is too close, suddenly moves, and if your dog gets STUCK at a choice point or goes OVER THRESHOLD...

* accelerated breathing
* up on toes
* intense stiffness
* pulling tight on leash
* unresponsive to handler, magnetized by trigger
* or any change for the worse...

GGRRRRRR
PERHAPS NOT SO SAFE A DISTANCE?

ABORT this trial by calling his name, making a sound, or shaking the leash to get his attention. Don't yell at him.

Move dog a few feet away with the trigger still in view or turn and walk away in the opposite or diagonal direction.

EXAMPLES:

BOOGIE!
VIBRATE LEASH
LET'S GO!
BUTT TAP
"KISS KISS" SOUND

TURN AND GO.
Avoid JERKING OR dragging, if possible.

RETURN TO STEP 1
Look at the trigger from a safer distance

* loose leash
* under threshold

INCREASE THE DISTANCE

Lili Chin image, reprinted from "Behavior Adjustment Training" by Grisha Stewart

Walks: Stage 1. Sometimes waiting for good behavior won't work yet in the real world. For example, the trigger is too close and the dog would be too stressed if you wait there. Stage 1 is the **easiest version of BAT**. Start off just by clicking the dog for noticing the trigger. Don't start with Stage 1 if Stages 2 or 3 will work. It's only listed first because it's the easiest for the dog. This is basically classical conditioning with a BAT flavor:

1. Dog notices trigger
2. Click
3. Walk or jog away (functional reward)
4. Reward with food or a toy (bonus reward)

Walks: Stage 2. When you can't control the trigger intensity (people or other dogs get too close, etc.), bring treats, so you can do the Bonus Reward version of BAT. The order of events is:

1. Dog notices trigger
2. Wait for alternate behavior (if possible), like looking away from the trigger, calm bravery, ground sniffing, shake-off, etc. Keep leash loose, and breathe!
   Note: If your dog starts breathing faster or looks like she's going to bark, say her name and walk her further away, so she can calm down.
3. Click
4. Walk or jog away (functional reward)
5. Reward with food or a toy (bonus reward)

Note that you *walk away before treating*, so the dog notices the functional reward. As time goes on, shift into letting the dog engage more with their environment. Begin to *do the set-up version of BAT out in the real world whenever possible*, using only functional rewards, not treats. Let's look at that.

Set-ups and Stage 3 Walks. Set-ups are ideal and should be part of your training program. Start with an easy version of the trigger and gradually turn up the heat. That usually means starting really far away from the trigger. Take breaks whenever the dog, you, or the helpers need one.

1. Walk toward trigger (or trigger approaches) only until dog just barely begins to pay attention to the trigger. Breathing should be fairly calm.

2. Wait for alternate behavior.
3. Say "Yes" right as the dog makes a good choice.
4. Walk or jog away (functional reward)

For more info on BAT, check out my book, *Behavior Adjustment Training*. You can also visit FunctionalRewards.com for some YouTube videos and links to the Yahoo groups for discussion.

This is just an overview of two ways to work on these issues—individual Monsters require difference kinds of approaches. There are other tips and tricks you'll develop along the way, like how to get away from Monsters (quick, well-trained, happy u-turns), not using flexi leashes, where to find Monsters to work with, tools like head collars or harnesses, etc., but this should get you started. Take a break, get some chocolate, come back tonight or tomorrow, and reread this section before working with your dog.

If you have a serious aggression issue, get help from a professional trainer or behaviorist. There are also a lot more tips in my other book, *Behavior Adjustment Training*.

Don't Leave Me! Preventing Separation Anxiety

Separation anxiety is a heart-wrenching problem, but full-blown separation anxiety is hardly ever seen. Dogs with true separation anxiety will not eat while their humans are away, except sometimes the furniture and even the walls! They will sometimes injure themselves while trying to escape.

Here are some tips to help your puppy or dog avoid separation anxiety, paraphrased from *The Canine Separation Anxiety Workbook, 5ᵗʰ Edition*, by James O'Heare.

- **Take time off when you get a new puppy**. Puppies under 11 weeks should not experience significant time alone. They should be gradually introduced to longer and longer periods alone. Keeping the puppy's crate in your room at night is a great way to avoid a lot of trauma for both of you. You can set it right next to your bed and put a hand in/on it to keep the puppy company.
- **Dogs new to the home should not experience significant time alone in the first seven days**. Again, gradually increase the amount of time spent alone, in preparation for going back to work. If you absolutely must leave the dog for an amount of time with which you haven't

conditioned her to be comfortable, here's a way to avoid backsliding: just before you leave the house, put on a strange, very visible hat. That way, your dog will associate the hat with the prolonged absence and your slow conditioning process will (mostly) survive.

- **Dogs show less anxiety if they spend their alone time in familiar areas**. That means that they should not spend the day in the basement or bathroom, if that's the only time they go to those rooms.

- **Arrivals and departures should be low-key**. Just say a quick hello or goodbye. That excited homecoming can wait for you to read your mail, check your messages, etc.

- **Leave the dog with a stuffed food puzzle,** like a Kong or homemade toy when you go. This keeps him occupied during that first critical half an hour while you are gone.

QUICK TIP!

The D.A.P. collar exudes the pheromones of a mother dog and can calm your puppy as well. Your vet may sell them or you can get them online.

I'll Be Home Soon, a short book by Patricia McConnell, Ph.D., has several useful tips. I highly recommend it for puppy owners to help prevent a mild case of separation anxiety from getting worse. Severe separation anxiety should be treated with the help of a professional and is often successful only with the help of anti-anxiety medication prescribed by veterinarians. They usually take about two weeks to take effect. Check with your veterinarian or a veterinary behaviorist to see if that's a good option for your dog.

A dog is an animal, a specialized wolf living in the human den, and not a furry little person—no matter how we view him. Simply because dogs live in our home and we view them as part of our family, most owners think we should be able to take a bone or any other item from our dogs at will. We become easily affronted if our dog decides to become possessively aggressive about his toys— even more so than if our kids become angry if we try to take their toys away! We can teach dogs that it's a good thing to give up their precious items, but that doesn't come naturally. Sharing their food and toys with adults (particularly of another species) goes against a survival instinct.

If your dog becomes aggressive about keeping her bones, toys, bed, or other objects, avoid thinking of the issue in terms of 'point scoring' or ulterior motives of long-term control of her human pack. Resource guarding is a safety issue for humans and a stress issue for dogs, but *it's a relatively easy problem to fix if you keep a cool head and avoid threatening your dog*. There is no need to assert your authority, folks! Don't be afraid of losing face or not being 'alpha' enough.

I feel compelled to mention this here because it seems like aggression directed at the owner brings out more dominance-based training than other problems. It's ironic, though, because resource guarding is very straightforward to fix without force. If you get pulled into a battle of wills with your dog over possessions, there's a big chance that you will make things worse.

So if dominance-based training isn't the way to go, how do we deal with a resource guarding problem? Here are some tips on how to teach your dog that having people around his stuff is actually a good thing.

Teach your dog the Give or Trade cue. Teach him to bring you everything that he currently guards to trade for treats. Start with objects that he does not value, like an empty cup or a boring toy, and rewarding with treats that are highly valued. Next, gradually work your way up to objects that he cares very much about. I'll discuss this behavior in detail later in the book, but here's the short version: Say "Bring It," "Give," or "Trade" and then either wait for him to do so (if he knows the cue) or put a treat near the corner of his mouth, which usually causes the dog's mouth to open and drop the item.

Reward and praise him for dropping the object, then give it back to him as soon as he's done chewing the treat. Practicing this cue, and being sure to *give the object back to your dog each time*, helps your dog understand that giving away his resources to a human is a good thing. I prefer to give the dog the item and then walk away, so he can enjoy it in peace. It's win-win for him, so there's no reason to guard 'his' stuff. Children should only work on this step under adult supervision. Start with the family member that the dog trusts the most (growls at the least).

Teach your dog the Off cue. If he is guarding the furniture, teach him to jump off of it on cue. Get him up on the couch by patting on it or luring him with a treat. Don't give the treat yet (we want to reward for "off", not jumping on the couch). Then say "off" and put a treat to his nose and use it to guide him back onto the floor. If you use a clicker, click as soon as he heads off the couch. Give him the treat. Don't start to teach off when your dog is all settled down on the couch. Work up to that level.

The Find It cue also works well as another way to get your dog off of furniture. Find It usually causes the dog to get up and jump off of the furniture to go look for his treat or toy. However, it's nice to have something that won't require food forever, so I teach the Off cue as well. You can use Find It (see Chapter 4) until your Off cue is strong enough to use even when your dog is asleep and snuggled under the covers on your bed.

Condition your dog to expect good things when you approach him, especially if he has some sort of highly prized resource, like a bone. As with Give, start with something your dog does not guard. Walk over, toss the treat while he's enjoying his low value toy or food, and then walk away. Do this with several low value toys throughout the day. Repeat this for several days until he begins to look up at you with a "Hey, she's here to give me a treat" expression on his face.

With the low value objects, eventually move up to touching the dog while he has the objects in his possession (in his mouth or between his paws). Touch him lightly, pop a high value treat into his mouth, and then walk away. Eventually work up to touching combined with taking the object (start by saying Give first), still feeding a high value treat, but now giving the object back before walking away. Over a period of weeks or more, gradually move up to repeating the above with higher and higher value items.

With the highest value toys/food/bones, start by just walking by the dog (out of the range that makes him growl) and dropping a treat. Move closer when the dog is ready; never progress faster than your dog is happily willing to go. This may take a few minutes a day for several days or may be done in a single session, depending on the severity of the guarding. If your dog is not relaxed and happy at each stage, you are pushing too fast, so retreat to the previous level. Repeat this entire process with several high value objects. After that, progress to doing this with more people around, more stress in the environment. Children should only work on the conditioning step under adult supervision.

Eliminate your dog's need to growl, freeze, stare, or show other resource guarding behavior by not doing things that push him beyond what he can handle. If he freezes and stares hard at you when you get within three feet of his toy, just move away. Until you have trained him to be comfortable with you approaching, stay more than three feet away from his toy next time, like double that distance or more.

Note: growling is an obvious sign, but there are less obvious signs of mild resource guarding, like stiffening up, moving his head over the food bowl to the side that you are on, or taking his toy into the crate. Another sign of resource guarding is turning his head away from you with his eyes staring at you, especially while lowering his head over the toy or food dish. Trainers call that threatening stare 'half-moon' eye, 'whale eye,' or 'stink-eye' and it's a sign that you are too close. A dog in that position is very likely to bite if threatened.

To be proactive, remove the toys that he guards from the living area, so that he can't accidentally be triggered. This is especially important if there are children in your home. If your dog guards his dinner, make sure no one gets too close to him while he is eating. You may even want to feed his dinner in a separate room until your training has time to take effect. If your puppy guards the couch, try to keep him off of it by not inviting him up and/or by making it uncomfortable to lie on. An upside-down carpet protector works well for that, just make sure the one you get is not too sharp. Any approaches that you make to your dog at this time while he has a resource should be on purpose and accompanied by a treat. Do NOT punish him for growling by scruff shaking or any other show of violence. All you will be doing is proving to your dog that he was right—humans are crazy and he's got to protect himself from them!

Keep it up. After your dog or puppy is happily accepting any human approach to his food or toys (a state that humans call 'normal' and dogs call 'strange'), you are at the maintenance stage. Twice a week, at first, then once or twice per month, approach him while he's eating, pick up the bowl, and plop in a handful of treats before setting it back down. Do the same with toys or bones as well. Occasionally practice the Give cue, replacing the surrendered object with something else if you really must take it away.

Oh no, he's doing it again! If your dog ever starts up again with resource guarding, it's not because he is trying to take over the world or that the training didn't work. It's probably because you haven't kept up on his training and he has started to notice that it's not such a good thing to give up his stuff after all. At the first sign that he's starting to guard his objects, remind him that humans are the source of all good things by going through the above process again—which should go much more quickly in the refresher sessions. This process is going to be easier on you if you begin working on rehabilitation whenever you see stiffening, freezing, etc. versus ignoring the problem until your dog growls or bites someone. In other words, when you see that first sign of stiffening around his food bowl, toys, etc., make a mental note to work on the problem right away. Start with a less-valued item, just like you did when you first worked on resource guarding.

My own dog, Peanut, had severe resource guarding as a puppy. I 'fixed' that problem using the techniques above and I usually need to work on some mild resource guarding every 2-3 years. His guarding comes out during times of stress or when I've purchased an especially good chew toy. For example, when I gave him his first raw meaty marrow bone, at 7 years old, he froze for a micro-second and lowered his head over the bone as I walked by. Talk about a valuable item!

He didn't glare, growl or snap, as he would've done as a puppy, but freezing is like the tip of an iceberg (no pun intended), so I didn't ignore it. I walked away from him and came up with a plan to work through the guarding again. Peanut hadn't shown resource guarding for a few years, but after he was done with his marrow bone, I went through the protocol I described above, starting with a plastic bone and then the marrow bone. He was soon bringing me a fresh marrow bone like a fetch toy and I haven't seen any guarding since then and he's now almost 10.

If you need even more help on resource guarding, check out Jean Donaldson's book, *Mine! A Practical Guide to Resource Guarding in Dogs* or better yet, hire a professional trainer or behaviorist who can help you learn to read your dog's body language and avoid getting bitten.

Prevention is easier than rehabilitation, so now that we know lots of ways to get rid of problem behaviors, let's talk about the ways we can teach dogs what we do want them to do. The more we build good habits in our dogs, the less effort we have to put toward stopping other behavior.

4

Good Habits are Hard to Break!

We are what we repeatedly do. Excellence, then, is not an act, but a habit.
—Aristotle

This is the longest chapter of this book, because building a solid set of skills is the main thing that you will do with your dog. I have included the standard behaviors like Sit and Down because they are popular to teach and it's important to know how to teach them using positive reinforcement training. I have also included Leave It and Touch because I think they are really useful for family dogs to know. The actual behaviors that are most important to you and your family may not be on this list at all, but my hope is that by seeing how to teach a variety of behaviors using positive techniques, you'll be able to extend this style of training to your situation.

If you learn nothing else from this book, please remember these three important points about how to get rid of or prevent any problem behavior: 1) "starve" the problem behavior (not the dog!) by removing reinforcement for the behavior, 2) teach your dog to do an incompatible or opposite behavior using reinforcement, and 3) change your own habits to reward your dog's new behavior with real-life consequences in order to make the better behavior a strong and reliable habit for your dog. Now let's get into the main course of this book: how to teach reliable behaviors.

Teaching Reliable Behaviors

Follow this general outline for any new behavior that you want to teach your dog:

1.   **Get the complete behavior** in some way (see tips on that for each behavior below). Click and reward each time the behavior is performed.

2. Once the dog offers the behavior freely and often, without prompting (in other words, it's starting to get annoying), you can **add the cue** (like Sit or Down).

   The cue is the signal that the behavior may possibly be rewarded. A cue is similar to what many people call a 'command,' except that with a cue, you are not demanding that, for example, your dog sit; you are only giving them a green light for the behavior. If she doesn't do it, don't force your dog into position, but also make sure that she doesn't get rewarded—either by you or by the environment. There is no need for punishment to make the dog fast and reliable in responding cues.

   For more details, see the section below on adding a cue to any behavior.

3. **Vary the reward schedule**: In the same environment as before, start to pick only the best performances (fastest sits, for example). Click and treat for about one in two. The one you click for gets double treats, given one after the other. Click and reward about five to ten times. For the times you do not click, release the dog with "okay" or "free" and praise the dog.

4. **Take the behavior on the road**. Dogs are scenario learners, meaning that they learn the behavior in that situation, but may not remember it in another place or in some new scenario. It's kind of like your dog is thinking, "If I am in this room, she has treats, and she looks at me a certain way, I get paid to lie down and put my belly on this surface."

Working in new locations can be a little confusing for the dog. Sometimes people expect too much, too soon, and get frustrated when their dog doesn't respond to the cue in a new location.

Expect to have to teach the behavior again in the new situation instead of being able to use the cue. It will usually go faster than the first time. After that, add the cue in each new location until your dog really has the cue paired with the behavior and not just the scenario. The same applies to times when your dog is in a new situation and seems to have forgotten the cue. Just retrain the behavior and add the cue again afterwards.

For dogs in training, 'forgetfulness' is part of the game—it's just a sign that the behavior isn't generalized well enough, i.e., your dog isn't fully trained yet. This shouldn't happen once your dog is trained, as long as you keep occasionally rewarding the behavior with real life rewards (see Step 8).

Practice rewarding the behavior while you are in different positions relative to your dog (like sitting, standing, lying on the floor, with your back turned, with treats out of sight, etc.). Also generalize your dog's understanding of the behavior by training in completely different places. Move to another room with a different type of flooring, but also practice out in the yard, on the sidewalk in front of your house, during a walk, etc. Have your dog do the behavior on different surfaces, like gravel, cement, or rubber matting.

Each time you change something that's significant to your dog, you may need to go back to step 1, but that's not the dog being 'dominant.' She just doesn't understand that new scenario! As you practice this in more and more places, your dog will progress faster. For example, at the 3rd or 4th new place, you may only need 5-10 repetitions before starting to click the best in two. Read the info about **choice points** below before you add a lot of distractions.

5. **Vary the reward schedule again**: In the same environments as before, start to pick only the best performances (fastest sits, for example). Click and treat for about **one in two**. You can start to

add duration at this time by waiting a few seconds before you click. You can also feed while the dog is in position, waiting a few seconds, then feed again while your dog is still in position, and then either click and treat or give your release cue. Expect that the dog will get up when you click. That's fine.

6. **Wean off of the treats & pay for performance.** After about 10-20 repetitions of #5 in the same environments, start to click about every **one in three** responses to the cue, picking out the best ones.

7. **You don't have to click any more in those environments**. Just release with "okay" or "free" and praise or give treats as the reward. Start to reward only about one response in four or five with food or toys. (See the discussion below on release cues).

8. **Keep it up.** Once you do about enough repetitions, responding will be a habit with your dog. New habits don't come in a day though, or even a week. Practice, practice, practice! If you go to the gym to get fit, there isn't a point at which you can say, "that's good, I'm in the right shape, now I can stop exercising for the rest of my life."

If you want your dog's behavior to stay strong forever, make sure you still reward in some way. That doesn't mean you have to keep giving him treats: you can use what trainers call Real Life Rewards. For example, if you're headed out on a walk, ask for one behavior and when your dog does it, say "yes" and clip the leash on. Ask for another and reward with opening the door. If you're going to give the dog something anyway, like a toy or permission to do something, you might as well use it for a reward at least some of the time. Just don't go overboard. Some things in life are free, so if your dog comes up to you for some loving, feel free to just do that. ☺ (If you or your trainer disagree with this, see Kathy Sdao's great book, *Plenty in Life is Free*.)

Choice Points—Set Your Dog Up for Success

Dogs learn better from rewards for good choices than punishment for wrong choices. That's even true of people, but it's more pronounced with dogs—they are worse at learning from punishment than we are.

A Choice Point is the moment where your dog has a decision to make about what she's going to do. If your dog makes a choice and she likes what happens, she'll probably make the same choice next time. Every day, your dog faces a TON of Choice Points. Do I chase that cat? Do I walk right now, or run? When Fluffy arrives at the intersection of Good Dog Street and Bad Dog Alley, which way will she go?

Your job is to set up the situation so that when your dog comes to a Choice Point, she has a good chance of making the right decision and getting a reward. For example, when you want to teach her to not jump up on visitors, start with a tired dog and a visitor she's just seen. That way, she doesn't develop a bad habit of jumping and then sitting, but just goes straight to the right choice.

Imagine if your elementary school teacher had introduced addition by asking, "What is 215 + 275" and if you guessed the wrong answer, he whapped you with a ruler? Even if all that he did was tell you "NO!" each time you had the wrong answer, you'd be a mess before naptime!

Instead, the teacher could start by explaining how to do 1+1 and then 1+2 and so on, and having you do story problems that you had a good chance at getting correct to give more breadth to your understanding of the meaning of addition. Noting the correct answers along the way would build your confidence in doing math.

Your day with your dog should be setting up a series of Choice Points and manipulating the environment so your dog gets it right. Gradually, you'll help him out less and less, and your dog will still make great choices! *Try to make it 90-100% likely that your dog will make the right decision at the Choice Points in her day.* Here are some things to think about when setting up Choice Points for your dog:

- How tired is your dog?
- How well does she know the behavior in this situation?
- Does your dog need some physical barriers to help make the choice? (Even when visitors come over, the dog can be on leash to prevent jumping, or baby gates can also help. On walks, you can kneel down and hold the collar.)

- Would having something else to do help her make the right choice? (Touching her nose to your hand when passing by another dog, chewing on a Kong when visitors come over, having other toys to chew instead of your pants when you get dressed in the morning, etc.)
- Should you step between your dog and the distraction?
- Should you move further away?
- How big/loud/close/fast is the cat/child/other dog?

If your dog does the wrong thing at a Choice Point, it's probably your fault for making the choice too hard. Take a 20-30 second pause (if possible) and think about what made your dog pick the wrong choice and make it easier next time. Set up Choice Points where the dog has an easy decision, both in terms of knowing the skill and wanting the reward that may come after doing it.

Just like people, dogs don't want to do hard jobs for minimum wage. Imagine these scenarios. Which ones make you likely to want to do this again next time?
- You clean a friend's house and she thanks you.
- You clean a friend's house and she takes you out to dinner.
- You clean up a crime scene and the police nod and show you out.
- You clean up a crime scene and the police thank you with flowers.
- You clean up a crime scene and someone hands you a check for $5000.

With dogs, the payments can be all over the map and they keep trying. However, when dogs are learning new and difficult tasks, they need higher pay! For hard jobs, like coming away from a group of playing dogs, surprise him with a big payoff every once in a while—for the rest of his life.

When you teach your dog a new behavior, the reward should be exciting enough that he's really interested in the training, but not so exciting that she loses focus. With my dog, Peanut, toys are way too exciting to teach most new behaviors, unless they don't require a lot of thinking on his part, like Come. If he needs to concentrate hard, as with agility obstacles, then I train the behavior with a high-value food treat first, and then once his behavior is precise, I can start rewarding with a toy to build up speed.

Adding a Cue to Any Behavior

The cue is the green light that tells the dog, "I am now paying for this behavior." Make sure you pick a cue that is very different than all of your other cues. A lot of our hand signals look alike to our dogs, and words like Down and Bow, sound very similar, for example.

Remember that the first step of training is to reward the dog enough for doing the behavior that he begins to offer it on his own. The phase of adding a cue to a behavior that the dog is already offering is like the game of Simon Says—the dog only gets the reward if you have asked for the behavior. For example, if a dog is throwing sits at me (i.e., sitting again as soon as the treat for the previous sit is finished), I add the cue by saying Sit (I am just be gambling that he is about to sit, at this point) and then clicking just as he sits. After the click, always give the dog a treat (in the general sense of the term treat, so it can be a toy). At first, click and treat *every time* your dog responds to the cue. If he doesn't Sit at this point, you are adding the cue too soon, so go back a step in the process.

If it is going well, though, then for some of the times that you know your dog is about to sit, don't say the Sit cue. At this stage, if you don't cue the Sit, you will not click or treat when your dog sits. Simply walk a few feet away or use a treat or your hand to lure him into the standing position. When your dog hesitates for an instant before sitting again, say Sit. When he sits, click and treat.

Repeat, gradually pausing longer and longer before you say Sit. The cue itself is a treat for his patience, because it means there is an opportunity to earn a reward. Once that is going well, mix in other cues that your dog knows, then say Sit and reward when he does. If he doesn't Sit, then you have just made things a little too complicated. Wait for a bit and your dog will probably sit. Then praise that but don't feed. Move to get your dog into a standing position, then cue the Sit again. Click and treat when he sits.

The rest of this chapter focuses on specific skills for your dog and activities that you can use to teach those skills. You can jump around to different behaviors or read through the whole thing for the clearest picture of what to do.

Name Game

Without using the name at all, I like to reinforce eye contact with a dog in training whenever the dog chooses to connect with me, especially if we are in a distracting situation. It is also important to teach your dog that his/her name means to look to you immediately for information on what to do next. Usually the name is a spoken name, but if you and/or your dog are deaf, you can just use a particular hand signal or a touch location that means the same thing as a name. Let's say that your dog's name is Peanut. If you have said it a lot in an angry voice, use a nickname, instead—either a brand new one or one already in use. Use a name that you don't mind saying in public. For sound-sensitive dogs, use a verbal marker, like "Yes," instead of the clicker.

Start off with your dog in a quiet setting:

1. Say his name *one time*, and then give him a treat. He doesn't have to look at you at this point, but he probably will look if you're in a quiet setting. Do several pairings of "Peanut" [treat]. Start to say it when he's not looking, then follow up with a treat.

2. Repeat Step one in several locations, inside and out.

3. Start to require that Peanut actually make eye contact for his treat. If he looks within 5 seconds of you saying his name one time, he can have the treat. Click to mark the moment or mark with your word, "Yes!" If he doesn't look at you in time, just step away from him, wait for about 20 seconds, and try again.

    If he doesn't make eye contact within 5 seconds the next time, then you're pushing too quickly. Go back to step 1 or work in a calmer, less distracting environment.

4. Move on to requiring that he look within 3 seconds, then 2, then 1, then the Whiplash Rule—only instant looks get treats.

The Name Game isn't my invention. I learned it from Leslie Nelson (author of *Really Reliable Recall*). She gives three reasons for the Name Game to fail:

    1. Icky treats. So use great treats!!

2. Not enough practice. Do 15 name-food pairings each day and surprise your dog.

3. Repeating the name. Say the name only once and apply whatever rule you were using. Put the treat away if your dog doesn't pay attention quickly enough, make a smoochy noise if you really must, but just DON'T REPEAT THE NAME! There is a statute of limitations on this rule: if a little time has passed and the situation has changed so that your dog is now likely to listen to you, go ahead and say his name again.

And remember, your dog is always learning from you, whether you think you're training or not. Every time you say the dog's name, he's learning what it means. Whether the name means "you're in trouble, run and hide," "the fun chase game is about to begin," or "pay attention to me" is up to you and your behavior, so *be consistent*!

Watch

When you say your dog's name, you are asking your dog to pay attention to you and wait for further instructions. For some dogs, I like to also have a cue that only means, "make eye contact" and isn't used in the dog's daily life as much as the name is used. I especially use this for dogs with fear, aggression, or impulse-control issues. As with the Name Game, use a verbal marker, like "Yes," instead of the clicker for sound-sensitive dogs.

To teach the Watch cue, first create a situation where it's very clear when the dog is about to look into your eyes. As with everything else, start this in a calm, quiet environment and work with more distractions as time goes on.

Have a toy or treats in one hand as a distraction. Your other hand is holding the clicker. Stand up straight with your eyes soft and squinty, hold the distraction out to the side, and wait for your dog to make eye contact. The dog can be standing or sitting for this exercise. Do not ask him to sit or prompt him to look at you—just be patient and wait. Your dog may jump, bark, whine, etc., but just continue to wait. The exception to that rule is if he gives up and starts to walk away from you. In that case, put the treat to his nose and put it back out to your side. That should bring her interest back, and you will return to just waiting. When he makes eye contact, click, praise him, and give him the treat or toy. Repeat that sequence several times until your dog starts to look at you right away.

When your dog has learned to look at you as soon as you put your hand out to the side, start adding the verbal cue. To do that, say "Watch" just before you think she's about to look (which should be just before you put your arm out). Still click and treat for the eye contact. Gradually start to wait for longer and longer eye contact before you click and treat. If your dog looks away, don't worry; just wait for her to look again. Start with something like ½ of a second and work up to about 10 seconds or more.

Begin using Watch at other times, with real distractions, not just the treat in your outstretched arm. Have a helper add distractions or use something from real life. Only say the Watch cue once. If it doesn't work, use a kissy noise or something else to get your dog's attention. Then when you have attention again, cue Watch and reward for a short instant of eye contact. Build up to longer eye contact with real distractions.

When the duration is good, you can start to give a release cue instead of the click. So you would say Watch and then after some period of eye contact from your dog, say your release cue and then reward with food, toys, etc. from some hidden location.

Recall Cue—Coming When Called

Getting your dog to come to you on cue is one of the nicest things you can do for your dog. If you are confident that your dog will return whenever you want her to, you can give her freedom to play and go where she wants to—within reason. The recall cue and Sit or Down from a distance are all skills that may save your dog's life one day, so it's worth putting some time into training your dog to respond quickly.

So how to build this solid recall? First, choose a word for the cue. If your dog is a puppy, you can choose whatever you want, just stick to it. If your dog is a rescue, you might want to pick something out-of-the-ordinary as your cue. She might have bad associations with Come from her previous guardian. Just test it out and she'll tell you. If she ignores you, that's okay. If she runs away, that's a sign you should use a different word.

Let's say that your recall cue is Come. If you have been trying the word Come for some time (and your dog isn't listening), do yourself a favor and pick a new word. The cue of Come, may be poisoned, meaning you or the dog's previous owners might have accidentally taught her that it means: "run and hide, bad things are about to happen." In that case, it's best to start fresh with a new word with no prior associations, such as Here. You want this to be one of the best words your dog knows. It means, "run to me, there's a party over here!" The idea is to never let your dog know that there is something better than coming to you.

- Things to avoid when training Come

Most of the time, my advice to people focuses on what they should do, rather than what not to do. That's similar to how I teach dogs—I focus on the positive. That said, you understand words, and verbally pointing out what not to do can save you some time and effort in your training, so here we go.

Never use the Come cue when you think your dog may not do it. At first, you may want to only say it when she's already on her way! Second, *never do something scary to your dog after she comes to you.* Scariness is in the eyes of the beholder, so what I mean is that when your dog comes to you when you call her, do not do anything that she does not like. That includes nail clipping, putting your dog's leash on to leave the park, or yelling at her for pouncing on the neighbor's cat. The last thing she did was come to you—you don't want to punish that, you should reward it! You'll have to be satisfied with telling her, in a nice, upbeat voice, what a rotten dog she is.

Don't add too many distractions or too much distance right away. Sometimes people can be too impatient when training their dogs. For example, they practice 10-20 times at home and think the dog "knows" what Come means. When I say to practice, I'm talking a hundreds of successful times before you start even adding in distractions! Practice success, over and over. Vary the location of the treats and the position of your body as you call. Much like underpaying the contractor building the foundation of your home, rushing the process or using punishment will likely lead to trouble in the end.

Finally, *never chase after your dog.* You do not want her to think that running away from you is a fun game. Whether she has a sock, you need to take her out of the park, or you just think it's fun, chasing is not the answer. You may need to run a few steps after her, but as soon as she notices you, RUN AWAY! Your dog sees movement better than still objects, and running away from her triggers her chase instinct.

- General tips for Come

The major steps in teaching the recall are to introduce the cue and then practice in a huge number of different circumstances, varying how far away you are from your dog and how enticing the distractions are to your dog. When you make one aspect harder, make the other one easier. You might use a long line for safety or as a gentle reminder of your existence, but don't use it to tug your dog to you. If you need the line very often, you are pushing her too fast.

Set your dog up for success. Remember the discussion about Choice Points?

1. Introduce the cue, Come, to your dog. Have a treat handy, behind your back, for example. Start with your dog right in front of you, so she doesn't have to move at all. Say the Come cue and then surprise her with the treat. Do that with different pause lengths, so only the word Come predicts that a treat is about to appear.

2. Do this somewhere where you know the dog will come to you. Start with your dog right in front of you. As time goes on, gradually add distance, like one or two feet away. In a friendly voice (not a command or a question, but an invitation), say "Puppy, Come" (the dog's name here is Puppy).

   Show her the treat and take a step backward. Stand up straight or even pivot away from her. Do not lean toward her. Leaning in is Doggish for "stop." Puppy runs to you, gets clicked for showing up, and gets her treats. Don't just feed one treat, but several, one at a time (only one click). Make it a real party!

   If she likes to be scratched, now is a good time. But be careful— she may not like petting at all times. Watch what she does. If she ducks away from your hand, now is not a good time or she doesn't like the way that you pet her.

3. Practice from further away. Do the same activity from 6 feet away. You say "Puppy, come," then get her to come to you somehow. She doesn't fully know the cue yet, so you want to make sure that she comes to you. Legal moves on your part are: waving the food in front of her face and running away; making kissy noises; clucking with your tongue; clapping your hands, etc. Illegal moves: walking over and grabbing her by the scruff of the neck, reeling her in with the leash, or in some other way making Come a scary word.

If your dog needs all those kissy noises, etc., you may not have practiced steps 1 and 2 enough!

- Treat Party—the emergency recall cue

4. At least three times a day, take a full 30 seconds to reward her for coming to you. Continue that procedure for a long time, at least a few months. I like to say a phrase over and over, like Treat Party, the whole time I'm handing out treats. Then I have an *emergency cue for come*. Say the Treat Party cue just when your dog is definitely coming to you, and then repeat it during the feeding or playing process.

I use the goofy cue of Treat Party because I want you to keep the parties coming, so that that cue stays strong, even if all else fails. Make sure you also remember to *say* the emergency cue in a real emergency.

For times when you just give your dog one treat, you can practice a few times in a row. To get her to go away from you, throw a treat and make sure she sees it fly. Then you can call her again.

5. Practice not luring her to you. When your dog has a clue about what Come means, start calling her without waving food around or making smoochy noises, from the same distance as before, or closer. If she doesn't start coming to you in a few seconds, make noise or get her attention and run away. Toss the treat to make her leave you, then call her as soon as she's gulped it down.

- Practice all the time

6. Practice as part of living. You can do this right from the beginning, but it fits in well at this step too. Call her whenever you think that she's about to come anyway. Reward when she gets there. Call her to you whenever you are about to do something good to her or for her. Feeding time is a great example. If you want to take her for a walk or let her out into the yard, those are great times too.

    If she knows sit, then you can call her to you, ask for a sit, and then do something that she wants: feed her dinner, let her out, or clip on the leash to go for a walk. Remember, **only call her for the fun stuff**; don't call her for bath time or clip on the leash to go for a walk if she's afraid to go outside.

- Gradually make it harder

7. Practice from even further away. Work up to ten feet, or fifteen, if she'll do it, all indoors, with low distractions. Reward generously.

8. Practice with distractions, closer in. Now make it harder for her by increasing the distraction level. We don't want to make it too hard, so have her closer to you, say 5 feet away.

9. Keep increasing the level of distraction and the distance until you have the recall you want. Make sure that, any time you call her, you are willing to do what it takes to get her to come to you. This may mean running away (one of my favorites) or running up to her, showing the treat, and then running away (safer method).

    It may mean waiting her out, which only works if she's not entertaining herself by not coming. If she's having fun, just go get her, calmly, or do something else to encourage her to come. Whenever she doesn't come when you call her, you have simply moved past her level of training, kind of like an athletic coach asking you to lift a weight that's too far beyond what you can safely lift. Just make the recall practice easier for your dog in some way and carefully build reliability.

- Treat fetching—A fun way to train and play!

Treat fetching is great for burning energy in a restless dog, with the bonus effect that you are training at the same time. In this game, you toss a treat out to make the dog go away from you, which sets up the chance for you to call him back again. You can do this inside on a flat floor or down carpeted stairs. There are lots of variations for this game, but here's the basic version:

1. Show your dog a treat, say, "Find it" and toss it out close enough that your dog will see it roll. (Toss further and further away during the session).
2. As your dog eats the treat, say, "Lola...(if necessary, do something else to get her attention)...Come!"
3. When Lola arrives, click and go back to step 1.

Variations on Step 3:
- Hold out a target hand (possibly saying "Touch") and click for the touch.
- Touch or grab the collar and click on contact, feed immediately, and go on to step 1 with another treat.
- When dog arrives, ask or wait for a sit, then click for the sit.

Another variation is to toss the treat, have a helper cover it up, and then you call the dog away from the treat. Click on arrival and say your release word (like Okay), then say, "Go get it" and point to the treat you tossed earlier. The helper calls the dog back and they get to eat the treat off the floor.

- More recall games

Here are a few examples of recall games that you can play with your dog:

Come & Go Get it - LOW distraction. Have a friend make noise to attract your dog over to him. After she runs over to him, call your dog. When you say your recall cue, your friend shuts down and becomes the most boring human that Puppy knows, so she will eventually run over to you, the interesting one.

Come & Go Get it - HIGHER distraction. Have a friend make some noise with a squeaky toy to attract your dog over to him. After she runs over to your friend, say your puppy's name and do whatever else it takes to get her attention, and then give your recall cue once you have her focus. "Puppy!!...Come!" When you say your dog's name, your friend shuts down and holds the toy to his chest, again becoming the most boring human that Puppy knows, so she will eventually run over to you, the interesting one. Then you give him a treat and run back over to the friend, who presents him with the toy and a fun game.

Come & Go Get it - possibly HIGHER distraction. Have a friend hold a container of extra-good treats and attract your dog over to him in some way. After she runs over, call your dog: "Puppy, Come." The friend then shuts down and holds the treats above dog level, yet again becoming the most boring human that Puppy knows, so she will eventually run over to you, the interesting one. Then you give him a treat and run back over to the friend, who presents him with the even better treats. Puppy learns that coming to you is the way to get what she wants.

Come & Go Get it - EVEN HIGHER distraction. When Puppy is playing with dogs, look for a break in the game and call her over to you. Give her a yummy treat and send her back into the fray.

Come & Go Get it - WAY HIGHER distraction. When Puppy is playing with dogs, call her over to you (the difference here is that she is actively playing). Give her a yummy treat and send her back into the fray. Be careful not to go past what she is ready for. You don't want her learning that she can say "in a minute" and go back to playing.

Come & Go Get it - SUPER distraction. Squirrels. You may never get to the level where Puppy will come running to you if you call her during a squirrel chase. There is a possibility that you can teach her to Stay or Wait so well that she will stop mid-chase. Then you can get her to calm down and, after a minute, call her to you.

Chase. Chase is only a good game when you are the one running away from your dog, because that's great practice for come (versus keep-away). Call your dog and then sprint away as fast as you can. She will catch you. Turn and run a different direction. She'll catch you again. Ask for a sit and give her a treat. You don't necessarily have to treat this one—chase is rewarding in and of itself. If you have mobility issues, a friend can hold your dog back as you move away and then release your dog when you call him.

Hide-and-seek. Hide in a closet in the house and call your dog. You may have to make a noise so she can find you, but don't make it too easy for her. Give her a nice reward when she finds you, maybe even a 30-

second party. You can play this outdoors and even at the park when she's ready for it. *If you go on a hike or to the dog park, play hide-and-seek whenever she gets too far ahead, say 20-30 feet.*

Two-dog recall. If you have multiple dogs, give a treat to the first one who gets to you. This also helps speed up responses to other cues. You can also treat the first one who Sits, Touches, etc. Just make sure that you feed in a way that doesn't cause a fight.

Relaxation On Cue

Most people are really good about revving up their dogs, without ever installing an Off Switch. Your dog can learn to relax on cue! The cue can be whatever you'd like, anything from a verbal cue, like Relax or Shhhh, to a smell cue, like lavender.

Start with no cue at all. You are going to shape relaxation. You probably want to start out with food rewards, especially in high-energy places like a dog training class, but eventually shift to petting, praise, and soft eye contact. You can sit in a chair and just wait for this relaxation or massage the dog and still mark the moments of relaxation. Use "Yes" in place of the clicker for times you're massaging. I recommend doing both methods. I will use the phrase "click and treat" even if you are using the Yes massage method.

Click and treat for any small bit of relaxation. At first, you want to be clicking every 5 seconds or less, so make sure to set the bar low for what relaxation means. You aren't looking for fully relaxed, just that the dog is more relaxed than he was the instant before. Click for blinking, looking down, mouth opening into a more relaxed position, sitting, lying down, tail moving slower, etc. Watch your dog at night when he settles down. Click every time your dog shifts a muscle into a more relaxed position.

Gradually, you'll start to get pickier, but you want to make sure that your dog is still getting a high rate of reinforcement, every 5 seconds or so.

Now you can bring out the lavender at the beginning of the session or start to add the cue. Try to say your cue right before you think the dog will relax; someone watching you should think your dog is already relaxing on cue, though they aren't. If you can't predict it well (you say relax and nothing happens), then you're trying to add the cue too soon.

As the sessions go on, you'll start with that high rate of reinforcement (every 5 seconds or less) but then gradually only click every 5-15 seconds, then 20-30, etc. At that point, you may be ready to switch to another kind of reward.

I highly recommend that you take your dog and a bunch of treats to the park, a bus stop, and/or a coffee shop and practice relaxation. The more you do, the better your dog will get at this. You can also do it right when you get home from work, which turns your appearance into a cue for relaxation. A miracle!

QUICK TIP!
You can add a cue to a behavior that your dog already does without asking. You just have to be clever to predict when she is about to do the behavior. To add a cue, just say the cue (or give the hand signal) right before your dog does the behavior. Repeat about 50-100 times.

To apply that tip to the Relax cue, just notice times when your dog is about to relax in her everyday life and calmly say your cue. For example, there may be a time when you are sitting on the couch petting her and she hears something outside. When you think she's going to settle back into the couch within a second, say your relaxation cue.

Sit

Sit has two components. Sitting from a down position is different to the dog than sitting from a standing position. We have to teach both.

To teach sit from a stand, put three treats in your right hand and the clicker in your left hand (vice versa if you are left-handed). If your dog happens to sit while you are getting prepared, click and give him a treat, and skip the next step (luring).

If your dog doesn't sit automatically on his own, use the three treats to lure your dog into a sit. Put the treats in front of the dog's nose and keep them close to the nose as you draw the treats slowly toward your dog's forehead, being careful not to lift the treats so high that your dog wants to jump. You shouldn't actually be able to get the treats to the forehead, because your dog's nose should follow the treats like a magnet. As soon as the dog's rear hits the ground, click and give one of the treats. Move a bit so that your dog stands up. Repeat for the other two treats, finishing up with the dog standing.

Now just look at the dog and wait expectantly. Yes, just wait. The dog has just earned food several times in a row for sitting. Dogs do what works, so he will probably try to sit again to see if it still works. He may just bend his back legs a tiny bit, sort of like attempting to sit. Click and treat that; don't wait for the whole sit. Keep doing that until you have a dog offering you lots of sits. To add the Sit cue and to make this behavior strong, go to step 2 in the training process and continue from there, including taking it on the road, adding distractions, and practicing Sit from a distance. Sitting from Down is similar—just use a treat to slowly draw the dog up into a sit. When you teach that, go back to luring without saying the cue, and then quickly move back into shaping.

QUICK TIP!

You can train your dog to do any behavior that she is physically able to do. If your dog has trouble sitting or lying down now, or develops that problem later, don't assume that she's just stubborn. She may be in pain, so never ever push down on the dog to get her into position.

Down

There are several ways to teach Down. One way that works for all dogs is called **Capturing** the behavior. Work in a setting where your dog is likely to lie down. You can do this by training in a small room with a seat for you (the bathroom works) or you can put a leash on your dog to keep him from wandering away and just sit on the couch. Next, ignore your dog by turning your head away and practicing relaxed breathing. Just as your dog lies down, click and treat. Toss a second treat a few feet away, so that he has to get up. Repeat this process until he is clearly lying down on purpose. Move to step 2 of the training process described in the beginning of this book.

Another easy way to teach Down is to use **Shaping** in combination with capturing. In both shaping and capturing, we use reinforcements to tell the dog what we like. I often do shaping over the course of several 1-minute sessions, but some dogs just need one or two sessions. Don't work until your dog is bored—stop while he's still into the training game.

Here's how to use shaping to teach Down. Have your dog in the sit position (I usually don't say Sit, I just wait for the dog to sit then reinforce it). Click any movement toward the floor, like head dips. Once your dog is dipping his head  toward the floor on purpose, as fast as he can, move to clicking for dips that are closer to the ground, say halfway. Next raise the criteria to touching the ground, then to holding it on the ground. We are gradually only clicking and treating for closer approximations of down. When the dog lies down, "jackpot" him by feeding about 5-10 treats, right after the other. Repeat.

One thing you might do before shaping is to use a little luring. Take three treats in your right hand and put the clicker in your left hand (opposite for lefties). You will use the treats to lure your dog into a Down three times, just like we did with Sit. With your dog in a sitting position, put the treats to your dog's nose and then slowly draw the treats down to the floor between his front paws, with his nose following the whole way. Slowly draw the food out along the floor, stretching him into a down. Click and treat for the down. When you do this, your hand should draw out a big L shape.

If you are having trouble getting your dog to follow the lure, just use shaping or capturing. If you really feel you must lure, it may help to wiggle the food a little, use stinkier/tastier treats, or click partway, while he is still following the treat, and gradually click for following the lure farther. Having your dog on a couch or a table can also help. Have the dog sit at the edge of the table, then draw the food straight down, past the edge of the table. Ask your instructor if you are having trouble with these methods; there are a few other ways to teach down that are hard to describe in this book, like luring your dog under your leg as you sit on the floor.

Release Words—Are We There Yet?

- Release cue

If your dog is heeling (walking beside you on cue), how does she know when to stop? When can she move from her stay? Can she go out the front door this time? Step off of the curb? Look away after being given the Watch Cue?

The answer is the release cue. The release cue tells the dog that they are free to stop the behavior, but you are not done with them. As in, "You can stop holding that stay, but I didn't say Go Play yet, so stay by me." You should say a release cue whenever any duration behavior is finished, including sit, down, stay, heel, wait, watch, and come. After the release cue, either continue working or give your end of session cue (see below).

Release cue examples: Free, Release, That'll Do, Green Light, Okay, Dog's Name.

So the 'conversation' with your dog may go something like this:
— Lola, Sit
— Gooooooooood girl (Slow, calm praise for sitting still. Sit has an implied stay.)
— Treat
— Goooood girl (Or say nothing, but pause instead.)
— Free! (Lola is allowed to move again.)
— Petting or click/treat (Call her back if she leaves.)
— All Done! (Lola is allowed to go be a dog.)

The one word on the list above that I should comment on is Okay. Why? It's a pet peeve for most trainers, but not for me. It's not the best choice, though, that's for sure. People say Okay a lot in conversation, so you might accidentally tell your dog that he's done staying if you are talking to someone.

But Okay is probably the most common release word out there. Even if you use other release words, your dog probably knows it, because you've accidentally used it as a release word. I have to confess, I use Okay with my own dogs, for that reason. I started out using That'll Do, but as it turns out, I often said, "Okay, that'll do" to my dogs. So Okay became my release cue. C'est la vie.

You can avoid confusion by picking a word other than Okay or making sure that you use a particular tone or make eye contact when releasing your dog. Okay is not terrible as a cue if you treat your release cue differently from your End of Session Cue. That way, the dog may get up, but without the end of session cue, he won't leave. Of course, you can't even spell Okay around your dog, like F-R-E-E, so it's a bit troublesome.

I really like using the dog's name in a sing-song voice as a release cue because I usually have more than one dog, and I may not want both of them to move. It's a tip that I got from Patricia McConnell, Ph.D., author of *Feeling Outnumbered: How to Manage and Enjoy Your Multi-Dog Household*.

To teach the release cue, you'll click and treat it, like any other moving behavior. It's best taught in a pair, like Stay/Free or Heel/Free. From a stay, you'll say your release cue and then click and treat when she gets up. If she doesn't get up, scoot your feet away from her or happily clap your hands and she will get up.

- End of session cue

All Done is the end of session cue that I use, but you are welcome to use whatever you'd like. All Done also has a hand signal, which looks like showing your dog that your hands are empty. I show the back of my hands and rotate both hands to show the palms.

All Done means "I have no more attention, rewards, or anything for you right now." It also can be used to tell your dog "stop begging at the table," "I see that you want to go outside, but the answer is no," "I don't want to pet you any more," or simply, "This training session is over." At ease, Doggie.

It's easy to teach. You just give the All Done cue whenever you are done engaging with your dog. Use it at the end of training, at the end of petting, etc. Next, ignore her. Yes, just ignore her, even if it breaks your heart. Look away and stop engaging with her. If you repeat All Done or look at her, you're just teasing.

The exception that I make to that rule is when I'm playing tug with a dog who is new to training. I might tug, say All Done, and when the dog stops tugging, click and treat, but you should quickly shift back to All Done meaning "game over."

Stay

Sit and down have built-in stays, because your dog is not supposed to get up until released with the click or the release word. That said, it never hurts to have a cue that specifically means "don't move until you are released." I like to practice Stay in the Sit, Down, and Stand positions, and once your dog has those, you can also extend it to other behaviors, like holding something in the mouth. For most dogs, it's just good to have one general meaning for stay.

Unless you are planning to compete in dog sports like agility or obedience, *your stay does not have to mean, "don't move a muscle."* Instead, it might just mean, "don't leave this spot," or "you can only get closer to the ground until you hear the release cue," so that lying down during a Sit-Stay or Stand-Stay is just fine. That is the rule I have with my own dogs—Stay means 'you can only move to a more relaxed position.' If I tell Peanut to Stay while he is sitting beside me while I'm talking to my friend, I'm more than happy to see him lie down and settle in.

To practice stay, your dog can begin in a Sit, Down, or Stand position (or any other stationary position, really). To teach Stay, give your dog a clear hand signal (usually a flat hand facing the dog, like a traffic cop might use for "stop."

Wait about one second and then feed your dog a treat. One second may be too long for excitable puppies and mellow dogs may find one second to be too easy, so use your best judgment on the amount of time you wait before treating. Staying for that amount of time should be relatively easy for your dog, because he has no idea what Stay actually means at this point. After you feed the treat, say your release cue and move around to encourage your dog to get out of the Stay. Click and treat when she moves, so she knows that moving when she hears the release cue is a good thing. Repeat this exercise. You can start to move around more while your dog is staying and also gradually extend the time.

The three variables to work with for stay are Duration, Distraction, and Distance (your dog's distance from you). The dog in the photo that follows didn't start as a fly-speck off in the distance. His training started with his handler just leaning back, then coming back to neutral and feeding the dog. Next, the handler stepped back and returned to treat. Each time you make one of the main variables of Stay harder, make the other two a bit easier. That is, if you work on distance, start with short stays and no distractions.

- Distance: Apply the **Goldilocks Rule**: Alternate between "almost too easy," "almost too hard," and "just right." You can reward each time and then gradually just praise and release for the ones that are too easy. For example, with a puppy who has practiced stay before, you might cue Sit, Stay, and then turn in a circle, praise calmly, return to facing your dog, and reward (that's the "almost too easy" part).

  Cueing Stay again at this point is optional, but I like to do that in the early stages to help the dog be aware of the cue through

Staying dog

  more successful pairings of the Stay cue and the dog staying. At any rate, next do a stay that is almost too hard (but is not beyond the dog's skill level). For example, turn and walk three steps away, return and reward. Then do a "just right" level of distance: turn and take just one step away, praise calmly, return, reward, and give the release cue. Good dog!

  Turning your body away is a big deal, so begin the stay exercise while still facing your dog and build up to turning away, walking fast, running away, etc. When you return to your dog, walk in an arc instead of directly at your dog. Having a human walk directly at them can be a little scary for some dogs. Added difficulty: more distance between you and your dog, less visibility (out of sight stays start with popping around a corner and coming right back), and mental distance (trainer focus on something else, like their phone).

- Distraction: Apply the Goldilocks Rule to add distractions like moving your hands, shuffling your feet, other people walking around (start at a distance from them), squeaking squeaky toys, other dogs being calm or excited, food being set on the floor, dropping food on the floor, tossing a toy, etc.
- Duration: You guessed it, the Goldilocks Rule. If your dog's average stay length is 10 seconds, then do a stay that's almost too easy, like 8 seconds, almost too hard, like 12, then back to 10. Note that the average of those three times is 10 seconds. Do several of those in a row and then move it up so the average is more like 15 seconds, etc.

If your dog moves before hearing the release cue, then his behavior is telling you that some aspect of the stay was beyond his level, so be ready to do another stay at which he can succeed. In the meantime, if he's on leash or in an area where he won't just run off and have fun, take a short training break, like 10-15 seconds. If that's not possible, just skip that step. Then cue for the position behavior again (sit, down, stand, etc.). Then follow that with the Stay cue and don't wait as long, add as many distractions, or go as far away this time, so your dog can hold the Stay until he is released. Reward your dog in position and release for making a good choice.

Set your dog up for success. If he breaks his stay more than once in a row, you are definitely expecting too much of him in the current environment. Make it easier and build up to excellence in an error-free way.

Wait

Dogs can learn a word that means "Don't leave this area or cross that threshold," rather than, "Stay in this exact spot." However, most people don't have time to train one behavior really well, much less, two. If you'd rather have only the Stay cue, the exercise below is mostly still helpful; just think of Stay when you see Wait and be a little pickier about motion.

You can use Wait for doorways, getting out of cars, and out of gates. No treats are necessary, although you can use them. Get set up at a doorway the dog wants to go through. Cue Wait and reach slightly for the door. If the dog waits, click and treat, or keep opening the door. The dog body acts as a switch—body not moving toward door causes the door to open; body moving toward the door causes the door to close. If the dog doesn't wait, close the door and when your dog looks at you, repeat Wait. Don't expect the dog to wait while you open the door all the way, at first.

Just go a fair amount, then say your release cue and let the dog through. Gradually require more self-control.

Use Wait whenever you can:

- At doorways to fun places, like your front door (he can't cross the threshold without permission, but the dog can move within the room while he waits to go out)
- At the food dish until you tell him/her to eat (dog waiting causes food to lower and dog not waiting causes it to rise up)
- At curbs and streets (means stop and don't cross until you say so)
- At the car (in case you need to load something first)
- In the car (you want dog to stay in car while you take stuff out or check traffic)
- At the top or bottom of stairs
- In the yard (wait in yard while you take out trash, for instance). It's best not to use stay for this until you've practiced a lot

Touch—Targeting Nose to Hand

The behavior here is that your dog touches her nose to a human's hand, but you can also apply this to a target of some sort. I'll use Touch as the cue in this example. You can use Touch to move your dog around in space or to get and keep your dog's focus. You can also use Touch to teach them to Heel nicely beside you, come when called, or move them from one side of the car to the other. The dog in the photo is being taught to jump through a hula-hoop with a lure, but you could also use your Touch cue to encourage the dog to go through the hoop. So if it's not clear already, I think that *Touch is a super-useful cue and should be a high priority for you to teach.* Once your dog knows it, you'll wonder what you ever did without it!

Start out with a treat and the clicker in one hand. You can have your target hand a flat hand or whatever you want, but I like to use two fingers as a target. Make a fist with your other hand, except put your pointer finger and middle finger out. That will be your visual cue for Touch. Present that hand to your dog. Your dog will then probably go toward your hand, expecting a treat. Ignore any pawing.

When she touches the hand with her nose, click and treat. While she's eating, put your hand behind your back and then present it again when you're ready to click and treat again. For some reason, it makes your hand brand-new and interesting again.

Do this several times before saying a cue. Once she's got the hang of it, and you're relatively sure she will touch your hand, start saying Touch right before you put your hand out. Continue to click and treat for touches.

If your dog stares at you and doesn't touch the hand, then either wait her out or put your hand behind your back and bring it back out again. Don't lean into her or stare (that's a bit scary). Your hand may also look like a hand signal you've already been giving her. If that's the case, change this to a new signal—hand flat, only one finger, etc. If she is biting your hand rather than gently touching with her nose, make sure you aren't clicking for the bite. Click sooner to reward her before her mouth opens, or click later, waiting for her mouth to close before clicking.

Begin to move the target a bit, so your dog has to walk a step or two to touch your hand. After this step, you're ready to use it for heeling. See Focused Walking, below, for how to use Touch to teach Heel.

Loose Leash Walking

Of the behaviors we expect a dog to do on a daily basis, this is by far the hardest thing to teach a dog to do. There are several different tactics that we use in our classes at Ahimsa. Forward motion is very rewarding to a dog, so the primary rule for leash walking is to *never let your dog move forward if the leash is tight*. Otherwise, we are rewarding them for pulling us. It's bad for their necks and it isn't much fun for us either.

Notice the difference in the pictures. The photo on the left is a tight leash and the photo on the right is a loose leash. While there is still some stress in the dog even after the leash loosens, there is definitely more stress in the photo on the left, even though the pictures were taken an instant apart. Use the list from the beginning of the book to get some information on the dog's stress level with the tight leash.

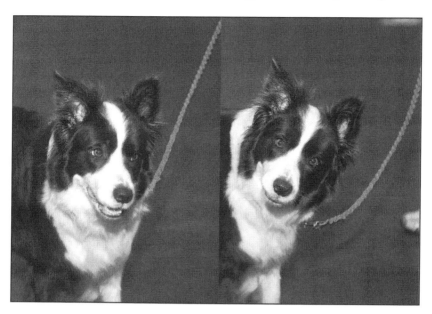

Think about where you want your dog to walk relative to your body. Out front? Unless I specifically ask for a dog to walk beside me, she can be out in front or behind me, just not pulling. Do you want them to walk directly beside you? When? Which side? Both sides? It's harder for dogs to learn to walk exactly at your side on both sides, but I think it's easier on their spines, and ours, so that's what I like to teach for a formal walking position. Your left side is the standard side for Heel (walking beside you), but you can have your dog do one side in one training session, the other side in the next training session, or have her start out with one side and then when you want her to switch sides, say Switch and lure her to the other side. I like having the Switch cue. On walks, if a dog is switching on her own to avoid something, please let her do it!

Some tools you might want to use are body harnesses with the leash hooked up front (my favorite is the Freedom Harness) or a double-ended leash. I also like using a longer leash (about 15 feet), but that takes some work to use. These tools allow us to have more control over the dogs. Avoid using the extendible leashes except for times when you won't encounter other people. To use them properly, get the "all belt" kind, which is actually a leash versus a little wire-type rope. Let out the amount of leash you want and then lock it. That way, there isn't constant tension on the leash, which teaches your dog to pull. You should also clip extendible leashes to the back of a harness, rather than the front, because even if you use it perfectly, there will be some reinforcement for your dog's pulling.

Here are some of the techniques that we use at Ahimsa Dog Training:
- o Click for Attention
- o Turn and Click
- o Focused Walking
- o Being a Tree or Backing Up
- o Speed Training
- o Penalty Yards
- o Silky Leash—a great technique!

- Click for attention / Click for position

You can teach your dog to pay more attention to you on your walks using the clicker. Start at home, where you don't need a leash. Training is all about changing the likelihood of behaviors. The goal of this exercise is to make "paying attention to my human" a more likely behavior for your dog. All clicker training exercises work best if the dog is not afraid of being punished for trying new things. That means that you can't really do well with this if your dog is on a prong collar. Focus on what your dog does right!

Step 1. Have an obscene amount of treats handy, in a pouch on your body or someplace nearby. You can use any reward your dog really, really loves, but food tends to work the best because it disappears quickly. Food treats should be small, stinky, and soft (pea-sized for big dogs, smaller for toy dogs). Whenever possible, I use healthy treats or a dog food brand that my dogs don't normally get because then I don't have to feel guilty if I feed too many treats. I just take it out of my dogs' daily calories.

Walk around the house with your dog. Each time she makes eye contact, click right as she makes eye contact and immediately give her a treat. As you feed, put the treat directly beside you, along the outer seam of your pants, so that your dog learns that that's a great spot to go to. Click for attention, or even the idea of attention: you are basically clicking right as you think she will look, so that the click sound coincides with the eye contact. The timing of the click is more important than how fast you give her the treat, but it should be within one or two seconds of the click. You should wait until the click sounds before moving to get the treat for your dog. If you move before clicking, then you've already promised your dog a treat and the timing of the click is lost. The click should be the only thing the dog notices from you at that instant.

You can toss the treat or feed in a particular location. The standard heeling position is on the left side, so I feed the treat about at my pants seam, on my left.

Click for every time she makes eye contact, right as she does it. Continue for one minute, then give your dog a handful of treats and stop. If you are getting great eye contact, continue on to step 2. If not, repeat step one until you would bet $50 that your dog will look at you within the next 5 seconds. If the environment is too distracting, try to make that easier for your dog and gradually increase the difficulty.

Step 2. In the next session, click any move your dog makes toward your left side. Imagine a big square on the floor at your left side and any time the dog steps into it or looks at it, click and treat. Try to definitely catch the times when she is on the left side AND looking at you. If you are in a quiet place, let your dog find the side; don't try to help her. If you just need to get going, then you can set your dog up to be successful here by moving around to get your dog on the left. Be sure to give her more responsibility for finding your left side or you'll create a dog that just sits there as **you** do all of the moving. Be patient! Again, keep the session short, about one minute long. Keep the rate of reinforcement high. That is, don't be stingy! Click often. Think of your dog as a teenager and yourself as a movie producer that has to keep her attention. After the click, give her the treat and praise her lavishly for focusing on you.

Step 3. After your dog has mastered the left side idea, then only click when she is on the left side AND looking at you, like the dog pictured on the previous page. I also really like how this trainer is holding the leash.

Next steps. Take it on the road! Repeat the two steps above on your walks. If you have trouble getting focus at all, you may want to practice in the back yard or in front of your house first. Stay on step 1 until you're getting good focus, then move to steps 2 and 3. After that, gradually extend how many times your dog must look at you for one click.

QUICK TIP!
The click is a promise of a reward! If you click, you owe your dog a treat, even if you clicked for the 'wrong' behavior.

- Turn and follow

Start your dog's training by doing Click for Attention, which I covered above. You can do Turn and Follow off-leash inside the house or outside on a leash (where your dog is probably still pulling some of the time). If you do this exercise outside, it helps to use a longer leash that is about 15 feet long. You can also attach two leashes together to form one longer leash. I also prefer that the dog wear a harness to avoid any pulling on the neck.

Let's say your dog is on your left-hand side. Have your right hand in the handle (holding the clicker if you can manage that) and use your left hand to draw up the slack in loops. As you are walking, pivot to your right and walk away from your dog. If your dog comes with you, click and treat as he turns to come beside you. If not, drop the loops of leash from your left hand to the ground. Click or mark with Yes when he turns to follow you or when he catches up to you. Feed the treat to your dog at the side seam of your pants. Loop up the leash again immediately. He may lose focus fairly soon, so gather up your leash to get ready to pivot away again.

When your dog is pulling (rather than just not focused) or if your dog runs into the end of the leash during this exercise instead of turning to go with you, let out leash slowly as you walk away, without pulling on him or allowing the dog to go any closer to what he was pulling towards.

As with Click For Attention, also click and treat when your dog is directly next to you or looking at you as you walk along. This exercise and Click for Attention are essential pieces of the training because you're showing your dog what you *want* him to do. Over time, you'll be clicking less frequently, but don't just make earning a click consistently more difficult for your dog. You might have this pattern (the numbers are the number of feet the dog walks next to you before you click and treat): 1, 5, 10, 1, 2, 15, 5, 20, 10, 1, 25,... The distance is increasing, but your dog doesn't always have to go forever between treats. This keeps your dog from

© 2012 Grisha Stewart, MA

getting a treat and then giving up and pulling because he knows it'll be a while before the next treat arrives.

This behavior will be called Heel (although it's not an official heel) or "close" or "with me," etc. Just like with everything else, you'll be saying the cue just before you know the dog will be walking nicely next to you.

In the early stages, you'll be using Focused Walking to get past big distractions rather than just hoping the dog will do something worth rewarding.

- Focused walking (Touch and you're heeled!)

This technique will help you teach your dog to focus on you instead of distractions. In particular, she'll be looking at your finger as you walk along (also known as "finger targeting" or "hand targeting"). This is great for getting past a distraction. Once your dog knows this behavior well, you can use it to walk past things that might otherwise ruin your lovely walk.

The idea is for this to be a fun, fantastic game for your dog, something you occasionally play on walks. I build up excitement first by asking "reaaaady?" to tell my dog we're about to play this or other fun games.

Start by using the instructions earlier in the book to train your dog to Touch your target hand on cue, even if you move the hand around. Work up to the point where your dog will touch the target hand, even if it's right beside you, instead of being in front of him.

Next, **Be a Moving Target**. After you have practiced Touch for a while and your dog is readily touching your hand, you can add movement. Present your hand and when your dog moves to touch it, back up so your dog has to follow you a few steps in order to touch the target. Click and treat when the dog touches the target. You can also move in a semi-circle while offering the target. The key is to get your dog following the target to touch it. If you have a short dog (or you're really tall), you can click for your dog looking at your target hand.

Now start rewarding your dog for following the target hand when it's beside you. It's going to start looking like Heel. If you want your dog to walk on your left, your target hand is your left hand, and vice versa if your dog is on the right. You might work both sides, but work only one during a particular session. Start by practicing this off-leash in your house. Say Touch and present the target hand with your arm straight down against your leg and walk a few steps forward. Wait for your dog to catch up to your hand and touch it. Click and deliver the treat slightly behind or precisely at the outside seam of your pants (never ahead of you). This ensures your dog doesn't surge past you and out of heel position.

While you're treating, say Touch again and continue to walk forward. As the dog catches up to you and touches your hand again, click and reward. You're heeling! After the dog is doing well at this, you can begin to say Heel instead of Touch, or say Heel and then Touch, if the dog gets confused.

Put Heel on a variable reward schedule by gradually spacing out the amount of time or number of steps between clicks and treats. I like to call this **Random Treating**: Increase every other interval. The numbers below can be seconds or number of steps.

> Ex. 3, 5, 3, 7, 4, 9, 4, 11, 5, 13, 5, 15, 6, 17, 6, 19,....
> (easy, hard, easy, harder, not quite so easy, harder still...)

Heel for a short time after each long stretch, so the dog doesn't notice the long pauses between treats are getting longer. You want to keep the dog thinking, "Maybe it's only two more steps before the next treat!" Note that even the short pauses are getting longer. **Random Treating works for Stay too!**

Once it's working at home, try it for a few blocks at a time out on your walks when there aren't big distractions around. If you encounter a bigger distraction, go back to rewarding more frequently or rewarding continuously. When there **are** big distractions, you can try the same technique, but put some extra-tasty food in your target hand, and make it easy for the dog by putting it to her nose and using it to guide her past the distraction. If that's not enough, pick up your pace!

- Being a tree or backing up

It's important that your dog not move forward when the leash is tight. This includes walking next to you on a tight leash. Forward motion reinforces pulling. Period. Unless you like pulling, you must never, ever, ever let your dog walk forward on a tight leash. (Okay, if you're escaping a fire or being chased by a pack of wild dogs, you can make an exception!)

If the dog is pulling in a direction that you want to go, you can do Turn and Follow. You can also just Be a Tree: stop and wait for the leash to get loose, then immediately walk forward when you feel the leash tension go away. The forward motion itself is the treat, so you can skip the food. Alternatively, you can Back Up: make a kissy noise and use the Mime

Pulling technique from the Behavior Adjustment Training book, also known as stroking the leash in TTouch®. With this method, you basically slip your hands along the leash as if you are pulling, and pivot away from the dog. It's pretty magical to see how little pressure it takes to get a dog's attention that way! When your dog starts to go with you, you can begin to walk in the original direction again.

If you see your dog running ahead, about to hit the end of the leash, apply the "brakes" slowly by letting the leash slowly slide through your fingers and gradually stopping the dog. Both of these options are negative punishment (taking away forward motion is a "loss"). It can help to say "eeeeeeasy" or slap your thigh a few times if you know you're about to stop your dog. Eventually, the word warns the dog that the leash is about to run out, so he slows down.

I find it's helpful to attach the leash around my hips, nice and low to avoid injury. Don't do this if you have a bad back or a dog that may injure you. You can also put it or around your shoulder like a sash, using a carabiner (rock climbing clip), although you should be careful if you have a big or strong dog. Don't just hook the leash to your belt loop, unless you don't mind ripped pants. I learned that the hard way! Until your dog catches on, expect some walks where you just don't get very far around the block with this method—for times when you must move forward, focus on using one of the other techniques to reinforce your dog with treats or toys for being in the right position. If you have a small dog, scoop him up and carry him to your destination.

- Speed training

This uses positive reinforcement instead of negative punishment. We have discussed using Be a Tree for times when the dog gets to the end of the leash. I have extended that technique into what I call Speed Training.

For this method, your walking speed will vary based on where your dog is in relation to you: the closer she is to Heel position (beside you), the faster he gets to go. Walk fastest when your dog is next to you in heel position (speed = 1) and slower as she gets farther away (speed =.75, .25, etc.). Slightly before she arrives at the end of the leash, you have the option of slapping your thigh or saying something like "easy" and if she reaches the end, either stop (speed = 0) or walk backwards for a bit (speed = -1) until she's focused back on you.

At first, the maximum Heel speed might be running—whatever pace your dog wants to go, so it's really rewarding. As the weeks go by, the Heel pace is gradually slower and slower to match our boring human pace. By inserting the word "Run!" or "Quickly!" just before you speed up, you can also teach your dog to walk fast on cue—great for intersections.

Several years ago, I used this method with my dog, Peanut, and lost 10 pounds. Seriously! He became my personal trainer. When we go trail running, I still run when he's beside me and walk if he's up ahead. He doesn't pull much any more, but on hills, I hope that he does, so I can use that as an excuse to slow down!

- Penalty yards

This is a great technique for all dogs, but an essential one for dogs that are too distracted to eat in public. It's meant for dogs that pull toward something in particular, like into the dog park or up to a person.

The Penalty Yards is best done as a set-up situation, as a way to really focus on the dog's pulling issues. After doing several Penalty Yards set-ups, simply backing up a few times on a walk can be enough of a reminder to snap your dog out of a pulling mood.

Set up a course that's about 20-30 feet long. On one end is your start line. On the other end is the finish line, which has something wonderful, like a helper with a baggie full of fresh chicken that the dog just smelled. The helper can rev up the dog, just not say any cues, like Come or the dog's name, because your dog is on a leash with you at the start line. The finish line can also be a squirrel in a tree that your dog wants to go chase.

Before walking forward, get your dog's focus by simply waiting or saying his name. Say your walking cue, like Easy or Let's Go. Start to walk forward. If the dog pulls off to the side, you need to make the end game more enticing or use his name or Silky Leash pressure to get your dog on the forward path.

If you see him about to pull forward (or he has already started), return to the start line. You can use kissy noises, slapping your thigh rapidly to make a little noise, or whatever else that is not painful to encourage your dog to come with you. The point is to reverse course, not to give a leash correction. You can also use the Mime Pulling technique I mentioned above.

Eventually, your dog will walk all the way from the start line to 6 feet from the distraction on a loose leash. This may take 20 minutes or more. While your dog is still being good, say your release word, like Okay or Free, and let him run up to the distraction and have a bite of chicken or sniff the tree where the squirrel was hiding. Gradually require your dog to go all the way up to the finish line on a loose leash before giving his release cue.

- "Silky Leash" technique

Silky Leash teaches a dog to pay attention to the feeling of pressure on the collar or harness. It's almost the exact opposite of being a tree. Use the techniques like Backing up or Be a Tree for when the dog is on a harness on your real walks. Practice Silky Leash at home on a collar until the dog is great and then combine techniques. This is hard to explain in words, so I highly recommend you watch one of the Silky Leash videos on the Ahimsa Dog Training website at http://DoggieZen.com/silkyleash (or search on YouTube).

So what is Silky Leash? That's the name I've given to a technique first brought to my attention by the online posts of Shirley Chong, an amazing clicker trainer. For the Silky Leash method, think of guiding your dog along with a single strand of silk. The basic idea is to put the tiniest bit of pressure on the leash and reward the dog for moving toward the leash. Dogs, like human toddlers, have a strong opposition reflex: if you pull on them, they will pull away. Silky Leash isn't about pulling the dog around, but it teaches her that any light pressure on the leash is a signal to move in that direction, rather than a trap from which she must escape.

Silky Leash has several steps. You will need to really follow this technique to the letter to teach your dog to notice the lightest flutter of your leash, even around big distractions. Until things are going really well using the Silky leash method, clip your leash to the front ring of a harness for your walks or attach a double-ended leash to the front ring and the collar, using only Silky Leash flutters for the collar.

There are two students here—you are learning to give instructions by leash very softly and your dog is learning to listen to them. If things aren't working, examine both students! *Stay at each step below until your dog is responding quickly.*

As your dog gets better at this, you'll start to practice on real walks, but at first, you will set up the whole situation so you have full control. In the meantime, walk your dog in a harness or some other type of temporary gear on any walks (or parts of walks) where your dog might pull.

Step 1. Sitting in a Tiny Room—dog takes one step. With a hungry dog in a tiny, non-distracting area, like a bathroom or exercise pen, set up a

"SILKY LEASH" TECHNIQUE

Silky Leash Technique teaches a dog to pay attention to the feeling of LIGHT PRESSURE on the collar or harness. The basic idea is to put the tiniest bit of pressure on the leash and reward the dog for moving toward the leash. Silky Leash has several steps and you will need to follow this technique to the letter. There are two students here: YOU are learning to give instructions by leash very softly, and YOUR DOG is learning to listen to them.

STEP 1: one step
(Tiny Room)

Click & treat whenever the dog takes one step in the direction of the gentle pull. PAUSE. Repeat.

STEP 2: two steps
(Tiny Room)

Same as Step 1 but click & treat your dog for moving two or more steps. Apply pressure a little longer than before.

This amount of pressure wouldn't tear a "paper leash" between you and the dog.

When the dog moves towards the pressure, move slightly away from him so that the pressure stays constant. Click & Treat. PAUSE. Repeat.

STEP 3: circle
(Tiny Room)

The goal is to get your dog moving in a full circle cued only by gentle leash pressure. Click and treat. Then repeat Step 2... PAUSE for longer; try both directions.

STEP 4: figure 8

Still in the tiny room, same as Step 3 but harder. The main lesson for the dog is to move in the direction of the pull until it stops.

STEP 5: bigger room "follow the leader"

LOOSE LEASH

(SIGNAL TO TURN)

CLICK! TREAT

You take turns being the leader! Alternate back and forth between following him and using a feather-light pressure to cue him to follow you.

STEP 6: out in the yard "follow the leader"

Same as Step 5, and practice zig zags, turns, circles, serpentines. When your dog gets distracted, flutter the leash and click/treat him for coming your way.

STEP 7: the real world

More distractions! Continue to have soft hands, flutter your silky leash, and click/treat whenever your dog follows your cue.

Big distractions? Take a wide arc around it.

Keep it up, Wean off treats and do NOT let your dog practice pulling between sessions.

Remember: YOUR DOG NEVER PULLS BECAUSE YOU NEVER PULL!

chair for you and have the clicker in your hand and treats accessible. I usually have treats in a pouch and the clicker and leash in the same hand (my right). The leash is attached to the dog's collar or whatever you eventually want to walk your dog on. The room should be small enough that when you sit in the chair, your dog cannot pull—the walls are closer than the length of the leash.

If a friend had a collar around your neck and had no way to communicate to you that she wanted your attention, you'd want her to pull lightly on the leash. Your dog agrees! Pretend that you have a raw egg in your palm, with the leash wrapped around it. Say the amount of pressure your normally put on your dog to stop him is 100; what we're looking for here is about 1 (so one percent of what you'd use to stop your dog).

Put a tiny bit of pressure on the leash. Keep the pressure low and wait. If your dog pulls away from the pressure, let your hand go with him, so that the pressure stays constant. Eventually, as your dog is not a frozen statue, and the room is small, he will move in the direction of the pull and the pressure will lower.

The clasp of the leash (by the collar) will probably dip down. Click and treat. If you are tired of waiting, you may vibrate the leash, just as a tiny chick's heart flutters. After each click/treat, give your dog a few seconds to pause and then put pressure on the leash again. I hesitate to use the word "pull" here because that sounds a lot more forceful than what you should be doing. Repeat, repeat, repeat.

Step 2. Sitting in a Tiny Room—dog takes two or more steps. Now you raise your criteria. Instead of just one step to ease off the pressure, we want more, about twice as far as your dog moved before! Remember that you are not trying to drag the dog around, but rather saying to the dog, "Move this way until I signal you to stop." You aren't putting enough pressure on the leash to *make* the dog move, just enough to signal that you'd like him to.

What you'll do is just apply pressure a little longer than before. So you pull lightly on the leash (no harder than before, remember, this is your friend!) and when the dog moves toward the pressure, move slightly away from him, so the pressure stays constant. As he takes the second step, stop pulling away. The leash pressure will become zero again and you'll click/treat. Repeat many times.

Shirley Chong wrote, "At this stage, it may well take the dog a while to notice the cue and respond. That is perfectly okay. For dogs who have been pulling for a period of time (YEARS for some of them!), it is going to take them awhile to re-calibrate what it is that they pay attention to." Be patient with your dog!

Remember, we're teaching your hands to be gentler, too. How are you doing? ☺

Step 3 Sitting in a Tiny Room—dog walks in a circle. If your dog is tall, you may have to stand for this step, but sit if you can. The goal for this step is to get your dog to move in a full circle cued only by leash pressure. Repeat Step 2, but now just wait longer and longer before clicking—ease off on the pressure later and later. Try both directions.

Step 4. Sitting in a Tiny Room—dog walks in a figure 8. Now we make the dog work a bit harder (and you!) by trying for a figure 8. Remember, you still want to have the finish be that the dog successfully got the pressure to go away and you click/treat for that. The main lesson here for the dog is that the pressure **means something** and that something is— go in the direction of the pull until it stops. Dogs have a natural reflex to go OPPOSITE of pulling, so we're fighting against that.

Step 5. Walking in a Slightly Bigger Room—Follow the Leader. You'll take turns playing follow the leader. Remember, we still don't want a sudden jolt of pressure, so you may need to follow your dog (gasp) during this time. This is the one situation where I allow dogs to pull on a collar. The room should still be fairly boring, so they don't want to pull a lot and small enough that you can follow them with constant pressure.

If things go awry at this stage, you probably didn't practice the earlier steps enough times.

So you follow your dog for a while (no pressure) and then put a tiny bit of pressure on your dog. Click/treat when he eases up on the pressure (right away—no figure 8's yet). If he walks into the pressure (i.e., pulls), follow him so that the pressure stays constant. Remember, this is supposed to be a smallish, boring room. Alternate back and forth between following him and then using a feather-light pressure to cue him to follow you. Gradually extend the number of steps your dog has to do before you allow the leash to go slack and then click and treat.

Step 6. Walking in a Slightly Bigger Area—Follow the Leader continues. This is where you head out to the yard. If you don't have a yard, you might ask to use someone else's house or an exercise pen that you've set up at a park, at least for the distractions. You want an area that you can still keep up with your dog in, so that may require cardboard boxes or ex-pens or something to make the area smaller. You can get fairly cheap temporary construction fencing from hardware stores.

Now you'll be "practicing having your dog do turns, zig zags, serpentines and circles while you walk relatively straight within the confines of your area." You are still clicking and treating your dog, as we've raised the criteria. If this setting is too distracting, practice more of this on Step 5 first. Don't worry if your dog is distracted some of the time; that gives you a chance to flutter the leash and click/treat for him heading in your direction.

Remember that we're imagining the leash to be a silken thread. It takes two to pull! You'll still need to follow your dog if he heads off so you can keep the pressure constant and occasionally flutter.

You should still be walking your dog in his harness or other Temporary Gear for most of his regular walks. If he is at the end of a walk and is not likely to pull, go ahead and attach the leash to his collar, instead of the harness.

Step 7. The Real World. Now you're ready for the big time. Continue to have soft hands, flutter your silky leash, and click/treat whenever your dog follows your cue. I would start with adding a few more distractions at a time, and walk in a place where it's easy to go in any direction, rather than only two. In the best of all worlds, you'd be able to walk right past any distraction. At first, though, you may have to do a lot of "Transitions." Transitions are turns and speed changes.

Big distraction up ahead? Flutter the leash and take a right turn, take a wide arc around the distraction, or gradually turn away and retreat. Click/treat your dog for following each cue. Super-big distraction? You might want to clip the leash back to the harness for that one.

Over time, you'll need to make fewer transitions and you'll be clicking less and less as your dog gains confidence and skill. You'll also be using more "real world" rewards, like squirrels in trees. The less your dog has practiced pulling before you started, the faster this process of weaning off of the treats will be.

More from Shirley Chong: "When walking your dog, remember the training principle of determining what your dog wants as a reinforcer and using that thing. If your dog wants to investigate the tree that the squirrel ran up, go there using transitions as needed; when you finally arrive, encourage your dog to investigate the tree."

Keep it up, wean off of the treats, and do NOT let your dog practice pulling on the collar in between sessions. Remember, your dog is always learning. Shirley writes, "And then everyone will tell you 'well, it's easy for you, your dog just never pulls!' You can just smile and mentally add the truth: your dog never pulls because you never pull."

Leave It

Leave It means "move your head away from that." Leave It is helpful for getting dogs to not eat a jar of pills that drops on the ground or even stop barking at something outside.

To begin, put treats in both hands (one is bait, the other is for reinforcing) and have the clicker in one of the hands, ready to click. The clicker hand goes behind your back and the other one will be the bait hand, which is shown to the dog. This begins with regular treats in your closed fist. The idea is to set up a Choice Point where the dog is very likely to leave the food. Hold your bait hand just far enough away that he's thinking about mugging you for the treat,

but doesn't. Just before the dog is about to turn away from the food, tell your dog in a regular voice (not gruffly or angrily) to Leave It, and then wait. Click and treat when he turns away from the bait hand, giving him a treat from your other hand. If he tries to bite at your bait hand during this exercise, you can either just leave it there (close your fist if your treats are on a flat hand) or say "too bad" and put the bait hand behind your back. As soon as he draws back away from you, bring the hand with treats back around.

Leave It means "this is off-limits until further notice." The only time your dog is allowed to have the item you told them to leave is when you explicitly say "Take It." At all times, you should set up a situation in which he is very unlikely to eat the treat and reward himself for not responding to the Leave It Cue. The training progression moves from treats that are impossible to get from your hand to food or toys that the dog could actually get if he knew how much quicker he is than you.

At first, the food is in a closed fist, then an open hand (be ready to close quickly). Next, the food is in a fist on the floor, then on the floor, ready to be covered by a foot. Next you might try risking it a bit, and get further away. After you are pretty confident in his abilities to Leave It, make the food more interesting. Other variations that make Leave It more difficult are food that he encounters on a walk, squirrels, etc. When you ask your dog to Leave It, don't use the leash to force him to leave it. Ask for him to Leave It and then wait for him to turn around. Click and treat when he takes his attention off of the distraction.

If he is taking forever to Leave It when you ask, then you can start walking away and get him to go with you, without rewarding because he didn't do it himself. If you find this happening often, it's probably because you need to work more at the lower levels and build up to the hard stuff, like chicken bones on the street.

So, to recap Leave It:
- Closed fist at dog level
- Open hand at dog level (ready to close)
- Closed fist on floor
- Food on floor alone (be ready to cover)
- Food on floor alone, further away
- Better food, run through the levels again
- "Found food" on walks

This should be an easy exercise for the dog, all the way through. If one level is too hard, back up and try a level in between the one that he did fine at and the one that's too hard.

Give or Drop It

If you are a dog geek, like me, your dog can learn the difference between Leave It (that item is off limits forever), Give (put that in my hand) and Drop It (spit it out). If you don't have a lot of time on your hands and don't want to teach a separate cue for the skill of dropping a toy, you can use Leave It as the same cue for this. However, if the item isn't permanently off limits, as when you fetch, remember to give the dog permission to get the item back using "Take It" or some other release cue.

> **SAFETY TIP!**
> If you have a child, I suggest using the word Trade as your cue, instead of Give. This models politeness and mutual respect. It reminds your family to trade for a treat instead of "stealing" the sock or slippers from the puppy, especially during the early phases of her training. This helps prevent possession aggression.

Here's one method for Give. At first, you are basically bribing your dog, but you gradually transition to him expecting a treat when you ask him to give, so that the toy or human item falls out of his mouth. At that point, you can start rewarding only some of the time, more like a slot machine than a coke machine.

Let's say he has a Kong in his mouth. First put the food right next to his mouth and ask him to Give. When he drops the Kong, click and toss the treat, so you have time to pick up the Kong. After he knows the Leave It cue, you can use it to keep him from going after the Kong once he drops it. If his teeth touch you at any time, the Kong should disappear and he should find himself alone in the room.

Next, hide the treat behind your back, ask your dog to Give, and then bring out the treat within a second, clicking and tossing the treat when he drops the Kong. Do this a LOT. Work up to two or three seconds between the cue and the food appearing. Repeat several times, staying at this level for several sessions and consistently giving him food for dropping the Kong until he starts dropping it after you say Give, but before you present the food. The first few times he does that, give him a jackpot and make a big fuss. After that, treat him for the times when he drops the toy on cue. On the other times, use the treat to open his mouth but do not give him the treat; tossing the Kong is enough of a reward. If you feel like giving him the treat, ask him to sit and reward for that.

Another way to teach Give is to have your dog on leash (so she can't leave with the toy), then say Give and turn your back to wait for her to get bored and drop the toy. Dogs are much more willing to drop something if they don't think it's about to be stolen. When you hear the toy thunk onto the floor, click and toss several treats off to the side, pick up the toy, and then give it back to your dog. If you wouldn't be able to hear the toy drop for some reason, you can use a mirror or the video camera on your phone to see behind you. If none of those options are possible, just turn so that you can still see but you are not staring at your dog.

Here's my favorite way teach Give. This is a great way to create a fast fetcher. Start with you and your dog or puppy in a long narrow area with few distractions, like a hallway or a beach. Have a toy that he likes enough to want to grab it off of the floor, but not so fun that he wants to hang onto it for dear life. If your dog is not so interested in getting a toy off of the ground, tug a little with the toy first to increase its value. Toss the toy toward one end of the area and immediately walk away from the direction your dog is now running. He should grab the toy in his mouth and try to zoom past you.

When your dog is about 4-5 feet away, click. You are marking the behavior of coming to you with the toy, even though that's probably not what he meant to do. Because the click means that a reward is coming, he's likely to drop the toy. Show him the treats he has earned and throw them a few feet away from the toy. I also usually say "Find It" before I throw food on the ground. Casually grab the toy and get ready to throw it again. If your dog doesn't drop the toy, when you click, simply walk away from the direction he's now running, and get him to chase you again. Click again just before he zooms past. If that isn't causing the toy to drop after several times, you either need to "charge up the clicker" a bit or use a less valuable toy. To charge up the clicker, you click and then treat several times in a row. Pause after the treat every so often so that it's clear to the dog that each click causes a treat, not the other way around.

After a short period of training, your dog will bring the toy back and drop it at your feet, but only because the click is causing him to drop the ball. Gradually start to click as he stops where you are (versus running past you), then only when his mouth starts to loosen up to drop the toy. Once the dropping part is reliable, you can start to say "Bring It" as he is running out for the toy and "Give" or "Drop" just before he drops it. After a while, you can click less frequently (about every other time), and fade the treats out even more as time goes on. For most dogs and puppies, the toy and the fetching itself become reinforcing, once the dog figures out the game. For some dogs, you may always need to pay for fetch. :)

Stop playing fetch with your dog before he loses interest in the toy. When you want to stop, give a few extra treats and put the toy away while he's eating.

> **QUICK TIP!**
> Don't play non-stop fetch with your dog! Dogs may get tired that way, but it is also very exciting and may lead to overstimulation. Look for other ways to exercise your dog or tire out her mind, like long walks, searching for treats/kibble in the back yard, or training tricks.

Tug Rules

There is a myth out there that tug causes aggression. It doesn't. If you are afraid your dog will bite you, or if your dog seems to get overly excited by tug, definitely stop playing. But I think tug is good for teaching the dog to switch between Crazy Dog mode and Thinking Dog mode. Spend some time tugging, following the rules below, then do some sit/down/stay exercises, then back to tug. Tug is also good for teaching dogs to control their teeth.

Tug should be played with the dog controlling how much tugging is going on. Don't break those little puppy teeth by lifting him up. You can go slowly side-to-side or just hold onto the toy. Be aware of your dog's spinal health: never tug up and down and don't give him whiplash by moving around too much!

1. The toy is yours. Not all toys, and certainly not socks, are tug toys. Have one or two special tug toys put away.
2. Tug starts on cue. The dog should not dive at the toy whenever she sees it. The tug game doesn't start until you say it starts. I use "Kill the Rope!"
3. Dog gives on cue. When you say Give, the dog should drop the toy. Teach Give using the steps below.
4. Dog Teeth on human skin end the game. If you're still teaching bite inhibition, follow the rules above. Otherwise, any dog teeth on human skin, accident or no, stops the game. Just drop the toy and

walk away. This doesn't work if your dog keeps the toy and spends 5 minutes tossing the toy about and gloating about his prize, but most dogs find the tug toy rather boring if you're not attached to it.

101 Things to Do with a Box

This is a shaping game in the spirit of the one popularized by Karen Pryor, world-renowned dog trainer and author of *Don't Shoot the Dog*. Karen is one of the marine mammal trainers that brought clicker training to the dog world. The goal is to improve your skills as a trainer and learn about a technique called Free Shaping. Originally, your goal for the dog is any interaction at all with the box. You can start to be selective once your dog knows it's about the box. This exercise is helpful for dogs that have been trained traditionally or generally need to learn to "think outside of the box." Pun intended, I'm afraid.

This game doesn't have to be with a box—you can use a milk jug, a basket, whatever, but generally it should be something that you don't mind your dog destroying. Have tiny treats prepared (soft, smelly, and small!). The treats should be uniform in size for easy delivery.

Have your clicker at the ready when you put the box down. Your dog will begin to offer behavior as soon as the box is there. If you wait too long, he may lose interest in the box and then there is nothing to reward.

Don't start with a goal for what behavior you will train; just see what you are getting and go from there. Click as soon as your dog pays any attention to the box. Things to click are, for example:

- Looking toward the box
- Turning toward the box
- Sniffing the box
- Stepping toward the box
- Jumping on the box
- Biting the box
- Stepping into the box

In other words, any movement "boxward" gets a click, and then toss the treat on the ground. The treat is used to keep the dog in motion. Try to avoid tossing the treat into the box—the dog *will* go put his nose in the box for the treat, but it's a more passive style of learning, and we want your dog to learn to think more on her own.

Do sessions in one-minute bursts. In between, pick up the box as you think about what to do next. If the dog is clueless that this is about the box, continue to click for any subtle motion toward the box in your next session. Make sure that your timing is on; click just before or during the action. If you're late, don't click—just forget about it and wait for the next chance to click. Clicking late will just confuse your dog.

When your dog starts interacting with the box in a fast-paced way, touching or looking at the box as often as it can, then you can start to raise your criteria. Select the interactions that you like and ignore the rest. For example you might select paw behaviors only. You can then start to be more selective, like only times when the dog's paw goes into the box (maybe eventually two, three, or all paws). Don't wait for huge leaps of progress; this is shaping. Your dog should be able to do behavior that earns a click very easily, every few seconds. If it takes more than about 10 seconds, pick up the box and see what you can do to stop being so picky!

Try not to move around, make smoochy noises, say her name, or otherwise do your dog's homework for her. Think of this as a story problem for your dog. Let her set up the equation herself, or she'll never be a problem solver!

Go To Your Bed

You can lure your dog onto her bed, but I suggest that you fade the lure (stop using food in your hand) after only a few repetitions. Better yet, use this shaping technique, which is eerily similar to the one that you practiced in the Box Game.

Behavior: your dog runs to her bed and lies down and will remain on the bed until released (shifting around while staying on the bed is okay).

- Put down the bed where you think your dog will feel comfortable. For example, avoid having it too close to a distraction or something that scares your dog.
- Lure your dog to the bed 3 times, clicking and treating when your dog puts at least 2 paws on the bed. This is not a necessary step, but if it makes you feel better, go for it, but no more than 3 lures!
- Now wait for any bed-ward attention.
- Click and treat as soon as your dog pays any attention to the bed.
    - For example, click for your dog's eyeballs glancing toward the bed, head turning toward the bed, stepping toward it, sniffing the bed, stepping onto the bed, etc.

- o After each click, toss the treat on the ground, off of the bed to keep the dog in motion and reset for another chance to approach the bed OR put the treat on the bed, and then lure the dog off with a second treat, which you don't feed him.
- After a one-minute training burst, toss a treat away. Pick up the bed and don't interact with your dog for just a bit, say 10 seconds.
- Put the bed down in several different places and repeat.
- When your dog starts to catch on, raise your criteria:
  - o 2 paws on the bed
  - o 4 paws on the bed
- Put the bed in several different places & repeat.
- When your dog consistently puts 4 paws on the bed, ask your dog for a down right at the moment you would have clicked (assuming your dog knows down) and click/treat between her paws. If your dog doesn't know down, you can either shape the down, ask for a sit, or work on more distance to the rug until your dog learns down in other sessions.
- When your dog is consistently going to the bed and lying down, be sure to Pay for Performance. Ignore or lightly praise slow responses. You get what you pay for, so pay for the work you would like to see. Sympathy clicks don't do your dog any favors.

- When your dog is consistently going to the bed and readily lying down, begin to delay the click. Treat her on the bed, although the click does technically let her know she's done.
- At this point you have taught your dog that the sight of the rug is the cue to go lie down on it. Now you're ready to add the verbal cue or a hand signal. Finally!
- Next, start to release her with a word and treat the dog for coming to you.

- Increase the duration of the stays using the Goldilocks Rule. (If you are doing this in a training class, you automatically have distractions around, so go slowly.)
- Increase your distance from your dog using the Goldilocks Rule.

LURING, SHAPING, CAPTURING
"Go To Your Bed"

Behavior: Your dog runs to her bed and lies down

LURING

You can lure your dog to her bed but it is best to stop using food after a few repetitions.

SHAPING

1. When your dog **looks at the bed**, CLICK & TREAT. **Feed your dog on the bed.**

LURE your dog off the bed without feeding. WAIT.

2. When your dog **puts 2 paws in the bed**, CLICK & TREAT. Repeat several trials.

3. When your dog **puts 4 paws in the bed**, CLICK & TREAT. Put bed in several different places, repeat.

4. **Ask for a DOWN.** CLICK & TREAT between her paws.

When your dog consistently goes to bed, be sure to **pay for performance.** Ignore or lightly praise slow responses.

CAPTURING

Whenever your dog goes to bed by herself

YES!
GOOD GIRL!
TREAT

ADDING A CUE

The cue is the green light that says to the dog you will pay her if she does the behavior. (No cue= no payment)

GO TO YOUR BED

Add the cue when the dog **already does this behavior** (trained with LURING, SHAPING or CAPTURING) but doesn't know what it's called.

Crate Training

Why should I crate train my dog? Dogs and puppies should all be taught to be comfortable in a crate or kennel. The crate is a great hangout place for dogs that are stressed, a fabulous place to go to avoid children, and excellent for safely taking dogs in the car (although I prefer safety-tested harness seatbelts).

Since your dog will probably end up being in a crate or kennel at the veterinarian's office at some point or another, it's helpful if your dog is already used to the crate. If you compete in agility, having a crate-trained dog is a must! Crates are also excellent for housetraining puppies. Dogs are much less likely to "go potty" in a small area like a crate. Puppies can't stay in the kennel forever, but it's a great accident-prevention tool.

> ### QUICK TIP!
> A general rule of thumb for how long a puppy can be in a crate is the puppies age in months, plus 1, so a 2-month-old puppy could stay in a crate for up to 3 hours if he has just pottied.

What kind of crate should I get? If your dog is not used to a kennel yet, you'll need a sturdy crate, not the crates that are made of canvas and mesh. Those kind of portable dog crates are good to have, but just aren't for newbies. The two main kinds of portable kennels are airline crates, like the Vari-Kennel, which are plastic and have a metal front, and an all-metal crate that looks a little scarier, but it isn't any more stressful on the dog. There are also fancy crates to match your decor. I have a wooden crate in my home that doubles as a table.

Choose a crate size that your dog can stand up and turn around easily in. The crate needn't be much bigger. For puppies, you'll either need to get different crates, block off part of the crate so the puppy can't pee in one side and sleep in the other, or use a crate rental service to avoid purchasing more than one crate. Your crate should have a nice soft crate pad in it. Some dogs will chew up their crate pads, so you might just want to use a towel or blanket. If all else fails, leave out the padding.

- Crate training option 1: shaping. So now that you have the crate, you have to convince your dog that it's the best place on earth. I like to teach this using shaping combined with a little luring at first. Put a tasty treat in the crate (that's the lure). If your puppy goes into the crate, click as he heads in and toss another treat inside. As long as he stays inside of the crate, keep clicking and treating. If he leaves the crate or if he doesn't go into the crate in the first place, follow the steps below.

- o Click for any attention toward the crate at all—even little eye motions. If your dog will go into the crate, put the treat in the crate and repeat the above steps. If not, just toss the treat a bit (not into the crate) to get the puppy moving.
- o Click several times for head turns toward the crate.
- o Click several times for moving a paw toward the crate.
- o Click several times for taking two steps toward the crate.
- o Continue raising your criteria (not paying for little steps, waiting for more).
- o Gradually start to expect the puppy to stay in the crate longer and longer between treats.
- o Briefly shut the door, click, treat, and then open the door. Before he moves out, say your release cue to tell the puppy he can leave the crate.
- o Gradually extend the amount of time the puppy is in the crate with the door shut.

- Crate training option 2: Go To Your Bed in the crate. Another option is to teach your dog to go to a rug and then gradually move that rug inside the crate. To transfer a Go To Bed cue to crate training, put the rug closer and closer to the crate until it's all the way inside. You can use the same cue or you can create a new one. Just cue Kennel and then pause for a second, and then cue Go To Your Bed (which your puppy already knows) and click/treat when she goes into the kennel and onto the rug. Eventually, train without the crate pad inside, if you want to make sure she's really getting the crate idea.

- More crate training tips. To add the cue, you can wait before the "run into the crate" behavior is strong but you can just start saying Kennel before she runs in even with a lure. To do that, just watch for when she gets the idea to enter the crate and say Kennel, so you are saying it just before she goes in. Say this every time she's headed in. She'll make the association after about 50-100 repetitions.

Don't do all of the crate training steps above at once. Train any activity, especially something as potentially stressful as crate training, for no more than about 2-5 minutes at a time. Between sessions, stop for play, naptime, potty, etc. If the dog or puppy begins to look nervous, lower your criteria and expect less from the puppy. Don't push so fast next time.

Once you can send the puppy in and close the crate door for a few seconds, give her bigger treats, instead of little tidbits. Kongs with peanut butter or wet dog food are great for this. Bully sticks or Nylabones are also great. Basically, something edible that takes a bit of time to chew on is perfect. Let the puppy out of her crate before she starts screaming. If your puppy does throw a fit, wait by the crate or put your hand into the crate, and when she *stops* crying for 5-10 seconds, praise her and let her out of the crate, or click and treat, then let her out. If she seems to really be panicking, i.e., claustrophobic and not just frustrated, let her out instead of waiting for her to settle and then make a big effort during your training to not push her over what she can handle.

SAFETY TIP!

Your puppy should not wear a collar or harness when left alone in her crate or pen. *She may get caught on the crate and strangle.* If you must leave a collar on the puppy, use something like a breakaway dog collar.

Leave your puppy's crate open to her during the day and hide treats or toys in there, so that when she happens to head into the crate, she gets rewarded. If you spot her heading into the crate at any time, say "kennel" (not so loudly as to disturb her progress) and either give her a treat or let her get the one inside the kennel. Crate training is a slow process, but it's worth it!

Helping your puppy learn to love her crate takes time and effort. In the meantime, you may need to use the crate because she's destructive and/or not housetrained. If you can at all avoid shoving the puppy into the crate before you've worked slowly up to leaving her in the crate for 15-30 minutes at a time, do so. That means that if your puppy is neither housetrained nor crate trained, you might want to tether the puppy to you with a leash around your waist or carry her in a front pack, which is a sort of marsupial pouch for babies that you can use with some dogs.

You can leave the puppy in the bathroom or an exercise pen with some newspaper for a few days while you train her to love her crate. In the worst-case scenario, you can use one type of kennel for leaving her in the daytime and train her to love the other one. At night, you can have her sleep in the bed for a few days while you train her to like her crate. For young puppies, it shouldn't take very long to get her to go willingly into the crate and stay there (though you may need to shut the door). Every time you put her into the crate, give her a treat that takes time to consume, like the aforementioned Kong.

Good Luck and Keep It Up

So now you have the basics of dog training! Hopefully you will have a chance to practice training with your dog at least 15-30 minutes per day, either on your own or in a group class with a trainer. If you only get one minute of training time in, don't worry. Any time you spend training your dog will help. Please just remember that your dog is always in training, so the more you can use real-life rewards for behavior you like and block the rewards for what you don't want, the more quickly and thoroughly your dog will learn.

Thanks for reading. Now go get yourself some sort of reward. ☺

IF YOU CAN'T THINK OF A REASON WHY YOUR DOG WOULD WANT TO LISTEN TO YOU, NEITHER CAN YOUR DOG.

Hint: "Because I'm the boss and his owner," doesn't count!

Resources for Even More Help

Here are a few of my favorite resources. There are more out there, too! As you search for books and other sources, always read with a critical eye, especially if the book has anything about dominance-based training or correction collars. For trainers, I do recommend watching and reading about all kinds of training so that you know what your clients have been through. The resources I am listing here are all progressive training.

Puppies

- *Give Your Puppy a Choice: Modern Socialization and Training* by Grisha Stewart (DVD)
- *Puppy Primer* by Patricia McConnell (book)
- *Control Unleashed: The Puppy Program* by Leslie McDevitt (book)
- *Way to Go: How to Housetrain a Dog of Any Age* by Karen London and Patricia McConnell (book)
- *Another Piece of the Puzzle: Puppy Development* edited by Pat Hastings and Erin Ann Rouse (book)
- *Your Outta Control Puppy* by Teoti Anderson (book)
- *Before and After You Get Your Puppy* by Ian Dunbar (book)
- *Perfect Puppy in 7 Days* by Sophia Yin (book)
- *The Puppy Whisperer: A Compassionate, Nonviolent Guide to Early Training and Care* by Paul Owens (book)
- *Quick and Easy Crate Training* by Teoti Anderson (book)

Aggression/Fear/Frustration

- *Behavior Adjustment Training: BAT for Aggression, Frustration, and Fear* by Grisha Stewart (book)
- *Organic Socialization* by Grisha Stewart (DVD)
- *Control Unleashed: Creating a Focused and Confident Dog* by Leslie McDevitt (book and DVD)
- *Fido Refined: Teaching Impulse Control to Your Excitable Dog* by Virginia Broitman (DVD)
- *Feisty Fido* by Patricia McConnell (book)
- *Cautious Canine* by Patricia McConnell (book)

- *Help for Your Fearful Dog: A Step-by-Step Guide to Helping Your Dog Conquer His Fears* by Nicole Wilde (book)
- *Chase!: Managing Your Dog's Predatory Instincts* by Clarissa von Reinhardt (book)
- *Guide To Living With and Training A Fearful Dog* by Debbie Jacobs (book)
- *Chill Out Fido: How to Calm Your Dog* by Nan Arthur (book)

General Training, Problem Solving, and Problem Prevention

- *Clickertraining: The 4 Secrets of Becoming a Supertrainer* by Morten Egvedt and Cecilie Koste (book with online bonus videos)
- *When Pigs Fly: Training Success with Impossible Dogs* by Jane Killion (book)
- *The Thinking Dog: Crossover to Clicker Training* by Gail Fisher (book)
- *Good Dog! Kids Teach Kids About Dog Behavior and Training* by Evelyn Pang & Hilary Louie (book)
- *Do Over Dogs - Give Your Dog a Second Chance for a First Class Life* by Pat Miller (book)
- *Bow Wow* series by Virginia Broitman and Sherri Lippman (DVDs)
- *The Dog Whisperer Presents Good Habits for Great Dogs: A Positive Approach to Solving Problems for Puppies and Dogs* by Paul Owens (book)
- *It's Me or the Dog: How to Have the Perfect Pet* by Victoria Stilwell (book, also a TV series)
- *The Toolbox for Building a Great Family Dog* by Terry Ryan (book)
- *Really Reliable Recall: Train Your Dog to Come When Called... No Matter What!* by Leslie Nelson (DVD and booklet, sold separately)
- *Hear, Hear!: A Guide to Training a Deaf Dog* by Barry Eaton (book)
- *Visiting the Dog Park: Having Fun, Staying Safe* by Cheryl Smith (book)
- *Off Leash Dog Play: A Complete Guide to Safety and Fun* by Robin Bennett and Susan Briggs (book)
- *Out and About with Your Dog: Dog to Dog Interactions on the Street, On the Trails, and in the Park* by Sue Sternberg (booklet)

Relationship and Getting to Know Your Dog as a Dog

- *The Other End of the Leash: Why We Do What We Do Around Dogs* by Patricia McConnell (book)
- *Canine Behavior: A Photo Illustrated Handbook* by Barbara Handelman
- *The Canine Kingdom of Scent - Fun Activities Using Your Dog's Natural Instincts* by Anne Lill Kvam (book)
- *Plenty in Life is Free: Reflections on Dogs, Training and Finding Grace* by Kathy Sdao (book and DVD)
- *Bones Would Rain from the Sky: Deepening Our Relationships with Dogs* by Suzanne Clothier (book)
- *Reaching the Animal Mind: Clicker Training and What it Teaches Us About All Animals* by Karen Pryor (book)
- *Love Has No Age Limit* by Patricia McConnell (book)

Especially for Dog Professionals (plus those of you who want to be dog pros and the rest of you who have caught the training bug)

- *The E-Myth Revisited: Why Most Small Businesses Don't Work and What to Do About It* by Michael Gerber (book)
- *The Human Half of Dog Training: Collaborating with Clients to Get Results* by Rise VanFleet (book)
- *Coaching People to Train Their Dog* by Terry Ryan (book)
- *So You Want to Be a Dog Trainer* by Nicole Wilde (book)
- *It's Not the Dogs, It's the People* by Nicole Wilde (book)
- *Teaching Clicker Classes: Instructor's Guide to Using Reinforcement in Dog Training* by Deb Jones (book)
- *The RCT Training Games Kit: Relationship Centered Training* by Suzanne Clothier with Heather Leonard (book)
- *Don't Shoot the Dog* by Karen Pryor (book)
- *The Culture Clash: A Revolutionary New Way to Understanding the Relationship Between Humans and Domestic Dogs* by Jean Donaldson (book)

Online Videos and Articles

- http://clicktreat.blogspot.com/2010/10/progressive-reinforcement-training.html Progressive Reinforcement Training Manifesto by Emily Larlham, to use as an ethical guide for training
- http://youtube.com/kikopup Loads of different training tips from Emily Larlham
- http://www.auf-den-hund-gekommen.net/-/Proof_Positive.html Great collection of progressive dog training videos from a variety of trainers
- http://dogwilling.weebly.com/videos.html Another solid collection of training videos from various sources
- http://tinyurl.com/7an5mjb Fabulous article about how the dominance model for dog training is sort of like believing climate change isn't real
- http://www.dogstardaily.com Constantly updated articles and videos on dog training

About the Author

Grisha Stewart, MA, is an author, seminar presenter, and dog trainer who specializes in puppy socialization and dog reactivity. She is a Certified Pet Dog Trainer (CPDT-KA) and was in the first round of students certified by the Karen Pryor Academy for Animal Training and Behavior (KPACTP).

She owns Ahimsa Dog Training in Seattle, which is a full-service dog training school that has earned many awards, including Best of Western Washington. Ahimsa has classes for family dog manners, problem solving, puppy socialization, aggression rehabilitation, agility, backyard sports, nose games, and more. Ahimsa also offers private lessons for problem solving, play times, and an intensive Puppy Day Camp for training and behavior modification of young dogs. This book is training manual and foundation information for all of Ahimsa's educational offerings. Exercises in the lessons from Ahimsa compliment the training advice found in this book.

Grisha has a Master's in Mathematics (Number Theory) from Bryn Mawr College. She taught university-level math, but her love for dogs won out and she opened Ahimsa Dog Training in 2003. Grisha is currently pursuing her second Master's degree—this one will be in Psychology with an ethology and behavior analysis focus.

Grisha's first career in mathematics serves her well in dog training and behavior consultations because she relies heavily on the problem solving, critical thinking, and teaching skills used in that field. As a dog trainer, she has found that her canine and human students are much more excited about learning than her college students were about math! She also really enjoys seeing the difference that education can make in the quality of life for her students.

Canine behavior fascinates Grisha and she is highly motivated to help improve our techniques for rehabilitating and training dogs. Her professional interest in reactivity, along with the need to find an efficient rehabilitation technique that would work with her own fearful dog, led Grisha to develop Behavior Adjustment Training (BAT).

Grisha's popular book, *Behavior Adjustment Training: BAT for Aggression, Reactivity, and Fear in Dogs*, was published by Dogwise in late 2011. It is available through all major outlets as well as http://FunctionalRewards.com

Thank you for reading!!

If you liked this book, please like our page on Facebook or
write a review where you purchased the book
http://Facebook.com/AhimsaManual

For more help from Grisha Stewart, visit:

DoggieZen.com/blog
FunctionalRewards.com (includes speaking schedule)
YouTube.com/ahimsadog

For help with your dog in Seattle, visit
http://DoggieZen.com

Made in the USA
Charleston, SC
11 January 2014